Better Blogging for your Business

A Guide to Creating Content to Build your Brand and your Business

Eric Miller

Copyright © 2017 Eric Miller

All rights reserved.

ISBN: 1976517818

ISBN-13: 978-1976517815

DEDICATION

To the creative people in my life. You have shown patience and given guidance to this engineer, especially those who corrected my spelling, patiently unwound my long sentences, and encouraged me to express myself. And indeed to my siren, calling to me with your song, onto the rocks.

ACKNOWLEDGEMENTS

This book was made possible because of the outstanding staff at PADT who helped make our company blog such an important part of our business and our marketing strategy. Also to Linda Capcara and Alec Robertson of TECHTHiNQ who finds the people that will take my writing, edit my diatribes, and promote our company's content across many different markets.

RESOURCES

Companion Blog

A book about blogging would be strange without a blog. So a small but hopefully helpful blog exists at:

betterbloggingforyourbusiness.wordpress.com

The site will share additional information that did not make the book as well as thoughts and observations about blogging and the process of publishing a book.

ABOUT WatermelonMonger.com

Throughout this book, you will find examples from an imaginary website, WatermelonMonger.com. There is no such company or website, but it is a fun example to use as a way to illustrate concepts in the book.

Table of Contents

Part 1: Introduction — 1
1. Why Blog? 2
2. Content Rules 7
3. A Look at What Blogs Are and Blogging Is 12
4. Understanding Your Goals 16

part 2: 10 Rules for Effective Blogging — 21
1. Publish Useful Content Often 22
2. Minimize the Cost of Production 28
3. Readability, Not Perfection 33
4. Be Concise 36
5. Stick to One Topic or Message 37
6. Write for your Target Reader 38
7. Link to Details and Background Information 40
8. Keep it Informal and Conversational 42
9. Use a Hierarchy Structure 44
10. Use Examples and Images 46

Part 3: Blogging Techniques — 49
1. How to get ideas 50
2. The Goal, Outline, Story Technique 56
3. Writing a "How-To" 62
4. Sharing News 64
5. Blogging about Events: Invites, and Recaps 66
6. Executing on Funny or Silly Posts 68
7. Getting Others to Create Content 75

Part 4: The Mechanics of Blogging — 79
1. Blogging Platforms 80
2. Templates and Styles 83

3.	The Built-in Editor	85
4.	Using Word Processors	87
5.	HTML Editing	89
6.	Dealing with Images - Tools and Techniques	93
7.	Tables	96
8.	Style Attribute and Tag	97
9.	The Sidebar	103
10.	Getting Statistics	105
11.	Plugins	106
12.	Embedding Video and Document Content	108

Part 5: Tips Becoming a Better Blogger — 111

1.	Look for Examples	112
2.	Form a Support Group	113
3.	Reread Older Content	114
4.	Raise the Bar	117
5.	Other Random Ideas to Make Your Blog Better	118
6.	Write	123
7.	Do it!	125

ABOUT THE AUTHOR — 127

PART 1: INTRODUCTION

Before we get into the details of blogging and how to create an effective business blog, it is important to establish some basic information and context for the rest of the book: why we are here, what the history of blogging is like, and what people look for in a blog.

1. Why Blog?

The arrival of the Internet, and especially the World Wide Web, has changed much about how people run their business and interact with customers. Regardless of whether your customer is a consumer or another business, the web has become a critical vehicle for building your brand and for influencing those customers. And, As with anything that is new and growing rapidly, there is a strong drive to make sure you are not missing out. Everyone wants to make sure that they are taking part in what is going on, that they show up to the party.

Blogging now falls into this category.

Many companies, especially small companies, feel they need to blog for no other reason than the fact that it seems like everyone else is blogging. Or they go to seminars or read content, ironically often in a blog, that talks about how important blogging is to the success of a business. And, as stated above, blogging is something they feel they need to do because if they do not, they will miss out.

Doing something simply because everyone else is doing it did not work well in High School, and it does not work in the business world. If you are going to spend time and money on an activity it is important to know what your options are, have a plan, and make sure that it adds value to your business.

Every blogging journey should start with the honest fact that blogging may or may not be right for your business. And, if it is right you also need to make sure you are getting value from your blog. The danger is that anytime you reach out to your customers through the web, you can very easily just be contributing to the significant noise out there.

To answer the question "Why blog?" we need to start with the basics. The first concept to get into your thought process is fundamental, why you communicate:

> **You communicate with your customers because you want to generate more revenue and you want to do so with the least possible cost to your company.**

Very easy to say. Hard to do.

Wanting to drive more sales and do so on the cheap are often mutually exclusive. There are a lot of ways to spend money that does not deliver any results. Also, like a lot of basic concepts, you often forget why you do something when you are nose deep in the details.

Once you have your head around the basics of why you communicate, you need to get a firm grasp on the importance of being effective. To be effective, you need to make sure you have value and are discovered:

> **Your communication with customers must be of interest to and be seen by the customer.**

You can create the most fascinating content in the world, but if it is not seen by your target audience, it is wasted. Also, you may pay a lot of money to put content in front of the right people, but if it does not attract and hold their attention, it is wasted. Both are needed.

The last basic concept to understand is really about marketing. It is addressing what the communication does:

> **Your customer-facing content must reinforce your**

brand, present a consistent message, and drive customers to action.

Once you do accept these three basic concepts, you need to find a way to achieve these concepts in a way that leverages the reality of modern interaction with customers. A reality that is heavily web-based.

Given all of this, blogging, when done right can be a very effective tool. Of all the web-based methods out there available to businesses, it is an avenue that is effective, simple, and something you can do yourself. But wait. Before you start sending out posts you need to understand all of the ways to achieve your communication goals.

We all dream of someday creating that meme, that video or image that explodes across social media and drives so many people to your website that it crashes. Unfortunately, that is the sort of marketing magic that tends to happen by chance. Keep dreaming, you cannot develop a strategy and a plan for a viral campaign. They happen and are not created. While you wait for it to happen, you need to find another way to attract people.

If you have a big enough budget advertising is a great way to go using various outlets including the Internet. Well spent advertising dollars can achieve the goals of building a brand and creating demand in ways that no other approach can. With the right team and the right message that is focused on your target market and appropriate to your industry, significant sales can be driven by advertising. If you are loud enough and if you are getting that advertising message in front your customers. And that costs money.

As many successful ad campaigns have shown, it does work. However, the reality is that most companies just do not have the budget, they cannot find that perfect advertising message, or they are in an industry that is hard to advertise in.

Another great way to get your message out there is through articles and stories online and in print. Yes, there is still some print out there, and most printed content is also published online. The advantage of this channel is that your target audience is actively seeking content through the channel, it is focused on your target audience, and you get credibility by being part of an established media outlet. As with advertising, having money to spend is the key to success with this approach. To get published by someone else you need to get noticed, you need to pitch your content, and you need to work a lot to get the message you need in the content. This can be even harder to do than good advertising because someone else controls what you are publishing.

So the viral meme is something you cannot force to happen, advertising is expensive and difficult to do correctly, and publishing through media outlets has the problem of not being something you control. This leaves you with the need for a way to communicate your message that fits your budget and that you control. And, given the name of this book, it turns out that blogging can be ideal for this.

Blogging is a buzzword for self-publishing content on the web. It is totally in your control, and it costs very little to do the actual publishing. The primary cost is in creating the content, and if done correctly, the cost can be small.

In summary, the answer to the question "Why Blog?" Is the following:

The fundamental reason for a business to blog is to address those basic needs of communicating with customers to generate more revenue in a way that attracts them and builds your brand while driving them to action.

2. Content Rules

People have been marketing on the web for some time, with huge growth during the dot-com bubble of the late 1990's that peaked in 2000. When the web was new people were trying anything to attract people to their websites and grow their business quickly. If you are old enough, you may remember the crazy Super Bowl ads in 2000. Fourteen dot-com companies had silly ads that cost on average $2.2 million each. This was when the industry crossed into the insane. The subsequent crash in 2001-2004 was partially brought on by companies spending millions on Internet marketing that did not produce results. Campaigns that were basically "Hey! Notice me!" did not work.

As the smoke cleared and people took a more serious look at the role of the web in marketing and sales, one thing became very clear – in the long run content is what matters on the web. If you want people to notice you, your content must give them value. That value can be a laugh, inspiration or, for long-term growth, information they can use.

The need for good content is essential to building trust and a regular following. But it is also critical for the most piece of the Internet marketing puzzle, search engines. The way most people will find your information is through search, and search engines are smart and are designed to give preference to what they perceive as good content.

In the early days the search engines were not very sophisticated, and if you wanted to rank high, you simply repeated the words people searched on over and over again, even hiding the keywords from the reader but putting them someplace the search engines can find.

Now is a good time to introduce a fictitious website that we can use for example:

www.watermelonmonger.com

We should imagine that it is a regional company that sells watermelon of all shapes and colors that is expanding into a national resource for watermelon lovers everywhere. Their goal is to grow their business without spending a ton on advertising, and they are leveraging their industry expertise and a blog to get their message out there.

In less sophisticated Internet days, if they wanted to be the number one online retailer of watermelon, they simply had to use the phrase watermelon in their text and buried on their pages. Using this tactic search engines might have ranked watermelonmonger.com high back in the day.

Over time the people designing the search ranking algorithms figured such a simple and obvious trick out, and they worked very hard to come up with ways to identify text that was useful content. As of the writing of this book, Google ranks content and links to that content as the primary influence on ranking. In today's web, watermelonmonger.com needs real content.

For attracting and keeping humans and to get the attention of the search ranking algorithms, pretty much everyone now agrees that "Content is King." But what does that really mean? What is quality content?

Unfortunately, this is a subjective measure, you know good content when you see it, but it's hard to describe. However, you can focus on a few key things to make sure content is good.

Substance

Content has substance if it is important, valid, and significant. It has weight to it, it is substantial. It is a good idea to take a look at each of those terms as they relate to a blog.

Something is important if it has significance or value. In essence, the information you provide needs to change perception or action of the people who read it. When you create content, you need to step back and ask yourself if someone will have an "aha" moment, or if they will say to themselves "this is the information I need to make my decision or fix my problem."

Making sure content is valid is a lot easier. The content needs to be correct and have a sound basis in logic or fact. This is critical because of the need for your readers to trust what you are saying. As with anything, you can make stuff up and hope people buy it, lots of sites do, but in the end, it is easier to just stick with what is real.

The hardest part of creating substantial content is making sure it is significant. Something is considered significant if the majority of readers consider it worth their attention and that it is worth remembering or saving. This is the most subjective measure of substance and requires some understanding of your target market to get it right.

If we are rebuilding watermelonmonger.com, we need to not just understand what people want to know about the fruit that is green on the outside and usually pink on the inside. Substantial content would include information on how to grow watermelon, how to cut it up, and recipes that use it. A great example of substantial information would be ways to tell when a watermelon is perfectly ripe. That is because it helps consumers make the right decision.

Expertise

Conveying expertise in your content is really about trust. It is creating the impression with your readers that you know what you are talking about and if they use the information you give them, they will know more and be better prepared than others. The thing to remember about expertise is that it is field specific. You may know a lot about tomatoes, but that does not make you an expert on watermelon.

The key to showing yourself as an expert with content is to find and share information that only people who study your topic know, and if possible more than most people who study the topic. For example, if you point out that watermelon has more Lycopene than raw tomatoes, you have conveyed a fact which the public does not know. This varies from substance because it is not general knowledge.

Useful

The definition of useful is "able to be used for a practical purpose." Determining if your content is useful is probably the easiest check to make. You simply need to ask yourself if your target audience can do something with the information you provide. Some people focus on content as being "actionable," meaning can the reader make decisions or do something with the information you provide.

On watermelonmonger.com, information about how to cook or preserve your watermelon is useful. The fact that it has a lot of Lycopene is also useful if you are looking for sources of strong anti-oxidants or if you need discussion material for a cocktail party.

Engaging

No matter how meaty or useful your content is if you present it in a boring or confusing way it will not be quality content. You need to draw your users in. Engaging content attracts and holds the reader.

Making something engaging is often just as much about how you present the information as what the information is. The proper use of graphics and story structure are the two most important parts of making content engaging. Images grab attention, the way you communicate keeps it.

A high-resolution picture of a juicy and ripe watermelon that leaps off the screen is an obvious way to make our fictitious blog site engaging. But once you have the reader's attention you have to work hard to keep it by presenting information they want in an easy to follow and understandable way.

3. A Look at What Blogs Are and Blogging Is

The term blog is a shortened version of Web Log. Back in the early days of the web (yes I was there, although I was not clever enough to do much more than watch) there were no good search engines and no tool to find things directly, so you spent a lot of time just exploring. And it was common to share with others what you found on your personal home page. It really was a small group of people exploring and sharing.

There is some debate as to where the whole concept of logging these adventures formally started. The consensus is that a student at Swarthmore College named Justin Hall starting logging his web adventures back in 1994 his page, Links.net. Check out the link, it is still there, and he still adds to it. It is a log of web visits but really was not identified as such.

Then In 1997 someone named Jorn Barger called his page, Robot Wisdom, a weblog. And as with most things, once it was named it was now a "thing." In 1999 Peter Merholz shorted it to just blog, saving us millions of "we"'s from being typed. On top of that, the words blogger and blogging sound better than weblogger and weblogging.

Much of this history is summarized in an article on the site webdesignerdepot.com[1].

---

[1] https://www.webdesignerdepot.com/2011/03/a-brief-history-of-blogging/

So here we were, the Internet was booming, and we had an excepted way for anyone to share what they were up to in small chronologically ordered posts. Accept it wasn't for anyone, you still had to create your own content using HTML and host it on your own website. Not ideal for anyone outside of computer nerd land. Seeing the need, a few people tried to create platforms, and they were OK, but still not for the average person who just wanted to type in some content and add a few pictures.

In 1999 Pyra Labs created a site called Blogger, which turned out to be what everyone was looking for[2]. It was simple, free, and searchable. Any user could spend a few minutes to write whatever content they cared about and put it out there. Others may read it, or they may not. The modern-day equivalent of the back room pamphlet press and town square bulletin board had been recreated and was now available to anyone with an Internet connection. Best of all, it could be seen by the world.

What we know today as blogging, the self-publishing of self-created content, was born with the platform. It can be a form of self-expression, psychological release, political speech, philosophical rambling, self-promotion, education, or marketing and advertising. For some, it has even become a profession.

It is a good time to stop and think about this: Blogging is truly revolutionary. It lets anyone say anything and make it available to anyone. Talk about free speech. Sometimes I wonder what our founding fathers would have done with such a tool.

---

[2] https://en.wikipedia.org/wiki/Blogger_(service)

But this book is about blogging for your business, so we will stop thinking about what Thomas Paine would have done with a blog, and go back to the principals behind it.

A blog requires two things: A platform and content. It is a good idea to take some time to really understand what both of these are so they can be leveraged properly.

To be a blogging platform, a tool must have the following:

- A user interface for content creation and management
- A reader interface for reading and searching content
- A simple text editor for creating content without having to know HTML
- A database that stores all the posts, images, and other embedded content
- Security so that only those that have access can create and edit content
- Runs on a computer that has web server software that is connected to the Internet.

There is a lot more in most blog platforms, but if you have these things you can create and publish a blog.

The other part, content, is what this book is about so let us just say that content is text, images, video, and other online documents that can be viewed through the platform. It does not have to be good, useful, or of interest to be on a blog. But it sure helps if you want anyone to read it.

Some attention should be given to the term Blogger as well. A blogger in its widest definition is someone who creates content on a blog. But most of the time someone is called a blogger if they get paid to create regular content, or it is their primary or secondary hobby, often about their primary hobby. As someone interested in blogging for your business, your goal is not to become a blogger per se, but if you did rise to that level, it would certainly elevate you to "trusted advisor" or "domain expert" status.

And of course, there is the term Blogging. Blogging is simply the act of creating content for a blog. Not everyone is a blogger, but anyone can take part in blogging. What makes blogging unique in human history, and it really cannot be overstated, is the fact that anyone can blog. You do not have to be part of a government, religious institution, publishing house, or media outlet to blog. And you certainly do not have to be part of your company's marketing or PR team to blog.

4. Understanding Your Goals

A section on goals in the Introduction to a book? That is a bit strange. But when you think about it, not really. Before we get into the meat of how to effectively blog for your business, we need to establish some foundational items. And goals are the most important of those items.

What is it you want to achieve with your blog? Stop right now and write it down. Do not worry about order. Brainstorm with yourself or with members of your team. A good place to start is to write down your overall company goals. If you have too many company goals, just pick the top three.

As an example, Table 1 shows what would be good goals for the Watermelon Monger company. They are in no particular order, just ideas based on the company's goals.

Once you have captured the goals, rank them. Leave out the company goals, just use those as a guide in your ranking. The purpose is to only end up with three to five, so a good first step is to split them into major and minor. Then rank the major goals. Table 2 shows a ranking for our made up online watermelon vendor.

Now you need to simply draw a line under the top three or four. Print this out somewhere or write it on a sticky note. As you work on your blogging, you need to use those goals to guide you.

Table 1: Brainstormed goals for watermelonmonger.com

- Grow sales outside of our state by 35% each year (Company)
- Average quarterly profit margin of 42% (Company)
- Keep marketing spend under 5% of revenue (Company)
- Be known as the best place on the web for watermelon
- Increase websites search ranking
- Differentiate ourselves from other melon and fruit selling websites
- Grow interest in consuming high-end watermelons
- Establish the WatermelonMonger brand across the country
- Reinforce the WatermelonMonger brand emotions of trust, quality, and natural
- Meet company profit goals
- Grow revenue quarter over quarter
- Increase watermelon sales in offseason
- Get the attention of the media
- Establish me as a domain expert for watermelon
- Build strong brand loyalty with repeat customers
- Increase social media impact
- Look bigger than we actually are
- Serve as a creative outlet

Table 2: Ranked Goals for watermelonmonger.com

1	Meet company profit goals
2	Build strong brand loyalty with repeat customers
3	Increase websites search ranking
4	Be known as the best place on the web for watermelon
5	Reinforce the WatermelonMonger brand emotions of trust, quality, and natural
6	Grow interest in consuming high-end watermelons
7	Increase social media impact
8	Establish me as a domain expert for watermelon
	Differentiate ourselves from other melon and fruit selling websites
	Increase watermelon sales in offseason
	Get the attention of the media
	Look bigger than we actually are
	Serve as a creative outlet
	Establish the WatermelonMonger brand across the country
	Grow revenue quarter over quarter

When you are about to write an article, looking for ideas for posts, or editing a story, refer back to those goals and ask:

Does this meet my goals?

How can I improve it to better align with my goals?

How much effort should I spend on this based on how well it addresses my goals?

Now you have thought about what you are doing and what you should focus on. It is time to dig deep into some basic but powerful rules for effective blogging for your business.

PART 2: 10 RULES FOR EFFECTIVE BLOGGING

Over the years, several hundred blog posts, and after teaching more than a few seminars on the topic of blogging for business, a few clear rules have emerged. The following list is certainly not comprehensive, but if you follow most of them, you will find that your blogging will achieve your business goals.

Most of these rules are based on where blogs have failed, even if they got off to a good start. And some are derived from looking at what has made a successful blog grow and thrive. Over time you may develop your own guidelines but still, you should find these basic ones of use to keep you on track.

As you read through the rules, you will see a lot of repetition. In fact, rules 3-10 are just ways to achieve the first two rules: publishing useful content often while keeping your cost down.

1. Publish Useful Content Often

This is the first and most important rule. You can skip all the others and still do OK if you do this simple thing. And it looks simple, actually obvious. But if you have ever tried to do a blog, newsletter, or podcast, you know it is one of those simple and obvious things that is very hard to do over time.

A good place to start would be to break down every word[3] in the rule:

Publish
  [puhb-lish] verb
  1. to issue (printed or otherwise reproduced textual or graphic material, computer software, etc.) for sale or distribution to the public.

The key part of publishing is getting it to the public. Writing a blog is not important. Thinking or planning does not get you anywhere. There is no value in blogging until something is sent out to the web. Clicking that publish button is when it becomes real, when it has an impact.

People can debate until the wee hours of the morning if a tree falling in the woods where no one can hear makes a noise. But there is no debating this fact: there is no value in a business blog post that is not published.

---

[3] dictionary.com

Useful
    [yoos-fuh l] adjective
    1. being of use or service; serving some purpose; advantageous, helpful, or of good effect:

The hard part when it comes to the term "useful" is determining what is useful. It is very easy to write about what you find interesting, what is easy to put together, or what has worked for others in the past. But is it useful?

You can publish words in a blog for the search engines to find, but unless your readers find what you say useful they simply will not read it. Your whole goal is to create a piece of information that makes them feel the act of reading was time well spent, that they got something out of it.

That "something" does not have to be technical information or some fact. It could be humor. It might be that you imparted some other emotion like empathy or even sadness. People seek writing that moves them, and not always in positive ways. You may simply help build a sense of belonging and community around your brand, and that is still useful.

If your company is a business-to-business concern, then "useful" is less fuzzy and more about giving your readers information they can use to make them more valuable to their employers, or help their business in some other way. You are still reaching out to a person, but that person's reason for reading your blog is simpler.

The easiest way to determine if what you are writing is useful is to look at the statistics on your blog. Are people not showing up? Are they spending enough time on a given post to actually read it? Sometimes you will have to experiment with different types of posts to see what people like or do not like. Also, your readers and what they find useful may shift with time. Reviewing the statistics on your site will help make these decisions.

It is also a good idea to try and guess at the usefulness of an idea before you write it, and while you are writing. Ask yourself if, given that you are a typical person that your blog is trying to reach, the idea would be useful. Would you find value in it if you find the content while searching the web?

Content
    [kon-tent] noun
    2. something that is to be expressed through some medium, as speech, writing, or any of various arts

Content is what we are here for. In the case of blogging, the medium is a web page on the Internet. And we are expressing something. The content we want to make is content that our customers, or potential customers, want to read.

The important thing to remember is that content does not have to just be paragraphs of words. That is the most common form, but it can be so much more. A good blog will include lots of images, presentations, videos, and of course, links to more information as part of its content. The richer the content, the more your users will get out of it.

It helps to think of content in terms of consumption rather than production. This is hard when you are the producer. Ask what attracts someone to consume the information you want to share, and what form best conveys that information to them. Think about how your target audience will access and share the information.

Even though this is the most important part of this most important rule, there really is not much more that needs to be said. The whole point of blogging is content.

Often
 [awf-tuh n] adverb
 1. Many times; frequently

You can produce the best content ever, the equivalent of the Great American Novel. But if you only put that content out there once your business blog will not be successful. Quantity is important. There are several reasons for this.

The first is linked to how the search sites work. They rank a site with popular and fresh content higher than one with a small amount of content that is not updated often. If you do not keep adding your ranking will drop. Remember, the purpose of the search engines is to find information that users want. If the content is not changing or being augmented, odds are it is not what your potential customer is looking for.

The other reason is that your readers, the customers, and prospects you want to attract, will not keep coming back. The whole point of having a blog, if we go back to the introduction of this book:

"The fundamental reason for a business to blog is to address those basic needs of communicating with customers to generate more revenue in a way that attracts them and builds your brand while driving them to action."

If you do not frequently add content, they will not keep coming back, and they will basically forget about you, your brand, and your call to action.

There is still one important aspect of "often" that is completely subjective and hard to nail down: who often is often?

Many factors go into determining how often you should publish. Finding the right balance should take into account:

- Your capacity to create content.
    If you set a schedule that requires content more often than you can produce, you are simply setting yourself up for failure. Pick a frequency that you can easily keep up with.
- The size of the content you create.
    Longer posts need more time between them than short posts.
- How often your competitors or partners wait.
    This is sort of an industry standard, and expectation that the people you are interacting with have.
- How information hungry your target audience is.
    If you are publishing to scientists, they like information and content and will tolerate a fairly frequent publishing schedule. If you are publishing to the general public, the truth is they are not that interested in a lot of information.
- You have to look like you are active.
    If someone comes to your blog and sees it's been three months since your last post, they will not take your blog seriously. If they see once or week, or even once a month, they know they can come here for up-to-date content.

If you are new to blogging and cannot use the above to help you, a good rule of thumb is at least once a month, and probably not more than once a week unless you have a large and diverse readership. If you have multiple contributors and multiple topics, three times a week can be maintained.

In the end, you need to use statistics from your site visits as well as feedback from your users to figure it out. But it needs to be consistent and enough to be noticed.

Publish Useful Content Often

Now that we have looked at each word in this rule, it is a good time to think about it as a whole. If you look at blogs that help drive business, they all follow this rule. They put out information that is of value to their readership, and they do it often enough to keep their interest. You have to make an educated guess at what is useful and what is often. If you know, your industry just use yourself as the typical customer. How often would you like to see content? What would you search for and find useful? Your readership and the business it generates will be the gauge you measure your success by.

This rule should be foremost in your approach to blogging. One way to make sure that happens is to write this rule on a sticky note or a piece of paper and put it on your terminal or on the wall by your desk, so you see it all the time. Then when you should be doing quarterly employee assessments and want something better to do, you will be reminded that you can create some useful content and put it out there.

Once you nail this simple but hard to implement concept, you will have figured out the most important rule in blogging for your business.

2. Minimize the Cost of Production

Remember that there are many other more effective ways to market your business. We are blogging because it is one of the least expensive methods. The whole value proposition is blown out of the water if you spend 40 hours of labor on each post. Controlling cost is critical to taking advantage of blogging.

If you can afford big money for advertising or content creation, hire someone to do it. Or do traditional activities and supplement it with blogging. The point is that if you spend a lot on blogging either in-house or with outside services to help you, you are taking away the value it provides.

The number one cost in blogging is going to be time. The website and software tools you need are free or cost next to nothing. Where you will spend money is the minutes or hours that are spent creating the content (which should be useful and published often…). So, when you look at minimizing cost you should be looking at reducing time to get that content up on your blog.

The most significant time, and therefore cost, is overdoing the quality of your blog. Quick and dirty is what you want, and for a lot of people that hurts. It is easy to worry a lot about how your blog looks, when in the end it really does not matter as long it is not a mess. Search engines do not care about formatting, nor do they give a damn about fonts. And the truth is most of your visitors do not really care that much.

So where do you draw the line? It is helpful to use other business tools as an example. A company car is a good one to look at. You do not want to arrive to pick up a customer in a car with paint flaking off, a pile of old papers in the back seat, and fast food wrappers on the floor. And you certainly do not want white smoke to be puffing out of the tailpipe. At the same time if you show up in a brand new German luxury sedan that has been detailed and is immaculate inside that may be nice, but it is not going to impress the customer enough to justify the cost of the car. At least for most businesses.

What works is an affordable and well-maintained vehicle that is fun but practical. You did not blow your budget on detailing or 18-inch rims. But it is comfortable, relatively clean and the few blemish add character rather than fears about safety.

The same is true of a good blog. Do not pay $5,000 for a custom template that has been color profiled, do not spend hours picking the perfect font family, and do not obsess about the spacing between the titles and byline. What you want is something they conveys a certain level of professionalism. I should convey that this is a business blog and not a personal or hobby site. It needs to be readable and easy on the eyes.

Aesthetics will be discussed in another rule, what this rule focuses on is quality and upfront investment. Use the "first impression" test. When you look at the site is it easy to read, look professional, and does not look "wrong?" If all of those are true it is good enough. Do not spend any more time, which is money, on it.

The next big time sink is research and preparation for posts. You are not writing a textbook or a definitive guide to whatever topic you are writing on. The key thing to remember is that you are sharing information with your readers, you are not trying to be a reference source. If you want to give more details, then you can link to references.

Beware, it is very easy to become ensnared in the process of doing research. It is fun, and you can get drawn in as your curiosity leads you deeper and deeper. That is OK for your own personal edification, but if you are getting paid to write content, then you need to have some discipline and spend only enough time to get the background information you need.

Once that upfront research is done, now comes the time investment to actually create your posts. In most cases this will be writing. It may also be creating a video or recording a presentation. Regardless of what it is you need to be fast. If it talks you twenty minutes to write a paragraph. Well, let's hope your employer has deep pockets. Or maybe you should find someone else to create your posts.

Creating the content should be fast and fluid. Try a more conversational approach, like you were talking to a colleague or sending a quick email to a customer to answer a question. Do not obsess about sentence structure or work to make sure you are writing in iambic pentameter. Your words should flow easily. Remember, most of your readers are scanning for information, not looking for a literary adventure.

How much is the right amount of time to work on an article for your blog? That depends on how important the article is and how much of an impact it will have on your business. Certainly, if you are spending more than six to eight hours to create a post, it needs to be an important and significant topic. If you are a normal writer, and not the type of person that can write paragraph after paragraph without stopping, one to two hours is a good time to spend on an average post.

Some will be much less. If you are blogging about some local news coverage your company got, ten to fifteen minutes should be more than enough to explain the event, include a link to the news article, and stop. Any more time is a waste.

If you are going to produce the ultimate how-to for your product, something that customers will use again and again, then maybe thirty to forty hours is a decent investment since this should become an anchor for your site. Most content will be in that one- to two-hour range for the actual writing.

Although writing takes up most of the time, an important part of creating your posts is including graphics. This is also where you can spend way too much time. Tools and processes to make this fast and effective are covered in a later section. But for now just focus on how critical it is to get good at grabbing, cropping, and sizing your images. I've seen people spend a day trying to get the right images in an article about a company team building event. Not value added.

After the writing and picking images you should invest some time in preparing the content for posting, but again, not too much. This is where you proofread and make sure your formatting is good enough. The most cost-effective way to do this is to actually have someone else do it. You know the content, and you will not catch the mistakes. Have someone else spend five to twenty minutes, depending on size and complexity, on a final check before you get the content out on the web.

Although this topic has detailed the steps needed for every post you make, it focusing on minimizing the time spent on each of those steps. The whole point of self-publishing is to save on the cost of getting your message out there. If you need to spend a lot of time on it, you should consider paying someone to publish it beyond your company to get a greater return.

3. Readability, Not Perfection

We covered this in the previous rule because the most common way that people drive up the cost of their content creation is to try and make their content perfect. This is one of those 80/20 rule situations – you spend 80% of your time doing that last 20% of formatting.

The goal is readability. You are not publishing a magazine nor is it a brochure. Remember, you are providing information to build a brand and deliver value to your potential and existing customers. This is done by making the information easily discoverable and digestible.

The easiest way to achieve this is to adopt an informal style in your writing that is heavy on images and sounds more like a discussion or a presentation than a formal article. That is so important it is actual rule number 8.

Organize your information into clear ideas and present them one at a time, using section headings and a single idea per paragraph. Remember that readability for someone surfing the Internet for information is often about skimming. Think about how you consume information on a blog. I ti highly unlikely that you get a drink, set up your favorite lounge chair, and spend an afternoon lost in a business post. You see it in an email, social media, or as the result of a search and you skim it for key information. Your readers will do the same.

If you happen to be one of those people that actually remember your English class, and it is not much of an effort, then stick to rules on voice, tense, and sentence structure. But if you are like most of us, doing that requires too much work. When someone reads a blog they expect a little less correctness and a lot more casual. Run with that to save time and get more content out for the same amount of effort.

Be warned, there will be grammar police and perfectionists that will send you sometimes nasty emails or leave comments about the fact that you switched from third person subjective to the first person possessive in the same sentence. Just remember that these people are the minority, and they probably have chronic indigestion or some other affliction that causes them to lash out at some poor business person that is just trying to build a larger customer base by sharing useful information on a regular basis. However, f you get a lot of complaints, you may want to find someone better to proofread your stuff. But if it is once in a while, it shows that people are reading your content.

This rule also applies to look and feel for your blog site. You may be tempted to spend a lot of time on creating a layout and color scheme that really stands out. Not only will this cost you more but in the end, it most likely will not have an impact on your readership numbers or the transfer of that reading into business. Keep things clean and simple. Use a simple and readable font, a white background, and colors consistent with your corporate branding. To emphasize your brand visually, use your logo and corporate color scheme. Your content will be the most powerful tool for building your brand, not fancy formatting.

The bottom line on this rule is: make it readable, then stop. Do not spend another thirty minutes perfecting things. Read it once and correct, then have your designated checker person read it one more time and find any other changes that need to be made, Then publish. When one of those grammar Gestapo people points out something, thank them, fix it, and update the post.

NOTE: If you are blogging for a large corporate company, sorry, this rule does not apply. Your posts need to be as close to perfect as possible. That last 20% matters. Make sure you budget for a professional copy editor and pay a graphic artist to create templates for your site look and feel that reflect your corporate branding. Some "their" instead of "there" is OK on watermelonmonger.com, not on multinationalchipmanufacturer.com. The expectation of the reader is different. Sorry, no pass for you.

4. Be Concise

This rule is easy for some and hard for others. Simply put, keep it short. Do not show off, do not repeat yourself, do not give elaborate examples. Say what you need to say and do not go on.

Unless you are doing a how-to that has a lot of steps, your posts should be 500-1000 words. News posts pointing to something else on the web should be shorter. If you are new to writing invest extra time in getting used to cutting the first dozen or so posts. Write what you want, then start removing content till you are within the right word count range. After you have done this a few times, it will be more natural.

It is perfectly fine to use a bullet list or three.

- Why convert it into one or more paragraphs when a bullet list conveys the information so well.
- It has the added advantage of being easy to skim and find on a page.

Getting that "aha, this is what I need to know" moment from a reader is business blogging success.

Having one sentence in a paragraph is perfectly fine if that is all you need to say what you need to say.

Why be concise? No one is going to read a long post. Get to the point, share the information, and stop.

5. Stick to One Topic or Message

The easiest way to dilute the value of a post in terms of search engine optimization and readability is to try to do too much in one post. Sticking to one idea per post meets our goals of conciseness, readability, and keeping costs under control.

Everyone creates content, especially written content, in their own way. Whatever method you use should include identifying the basic idea you want to convey then sticking to that one topic. The simplest way to do that is to put the idea in the title.

When you do happen to finish a piece and realize you have actually covered two or more topics rejoice. This is a good thing. Now you have two or more posts. Split it up and create a series. The advantage of a series is you can link them together, creating better traffic on your site.

Some good tools for picking topics and making sure you only address one, are discussed in Blogging Techniques.

6. Write for your Target Reader

When you create a blog for your business, unless you work for a gigantic retailer, you are trying to target a specific market – your customer base. It therefore makes perfect sense to work very hard at creating content (which you publish often and that is useful) that is for that market. It is an advantage and at the same time a struggle.

The advantage is that you should know your industry and the type of people who are the target in the market. The struggle is understanding who you really want to reach. You can cast a wide net, or you can shoot for the prospects that are easiest to create content for. But are they your target reader?

A good place to start is defining your personas, a fairly typical marketing task that someone in your company should have already done. If not, you should take some time to figure the personas out. Even if you have a blog that has been out there for a while, it is a good idea to understand what your potential customers look like.

After you have personas, the hard part happens. Which of those people should you target? You are looking for people that will increase your business through interacting with your blog. You want people who can make decisions about paying you money for whatever it is you do or sell, or influence those who can.

A good rule of thumb is to pick between one and four personas to create content for. Then you need to determine what types of content those personas are interested in and more importantly what can turn that interest into action.

When you are discussing a story idea with co-workers, and someone says: "I don't think Marge will like this, but Tyler will love it" you know you have made personas part of your process. If that sentence makes no sense to you, go research personas in marketing.

Now you are armed with who you need to speak to. The next step is to keep personas in mind as you are creating your posts. It is not a bad idea when planning your post out to jot down who the target is and what they care about.

Once you start attempting to match content to people you should follow up and see how well you are doing. Reach out to your readers for feedback or talk to readers when you meet them. A little bit of feedback can go a long way.

7. Link to Details and Background Information

The whole point of HTML, the HyperText Markup Language, is to provide a consistent way to link objects in one part of the document to a different part or to an entirely different document. Yet many bloggers get busy creating content and forget about links. They are your friend on many different levels, treat them as such. Get to know them, understand them, help them be more effective, and take advantage of them.

The primary reason why you should use links to details and background information is that search engines like this. If you link to a popular location as well as to multiple locations that are related through their own links, your post is starting to look like it is part of a larger thing. This will rank you higher.

Using links also achieves the important rule of being concise. Do not repeat information that is available elsewhere, just include what users will want easy access to. If they want more, they can simply click. This keeps your articles fresh and to the point without hiding access to more stuff.

A more subtle advantage of including links is to not look like a know-it-all. If your readers know anything about the topic you are writing about, they will not appreciate you making it look like you are originating well-known information. Or worse, that you are just making it up. Linking to other sites provides credibility and credit where credit is due.

Which brings up the topic of citing sources. Unless you are writing an academic paper, you really do not have to provide a formal bibliography. What you should do is default to the just mentioned idea of giving credit to people that deserve it. Instead of formal footnotes, you should provide links to where you got your information or include a list of "sites with more information that were used in creating this post" at the bottom of your post.

Here are some recommendations for content you provide links for as reference or instead of providing details:

- Definitions of keywords
- Sources
- A link to details or more information that is really outside of the scope of the article, but that your readers might find useful
- Background information that people familiar with your topic should already know, but that people new to the subject should know.
- Related content that readers may also find useful, especially if it is content you wrote.
- Documents that help convey the information you want to share; things like slideshows, videos, white papers, etc.... Although, the advantage of embedding this information will be covered in Tools for Blogging.

One of the reasons why some people avoid links is they are afraid that their readers will go off to another site and they will lose them. This is a valid concern, but it should not stop you. Make sure you set the options on your link to open the link in a new tab or page. Beyond that, the only way to keep people on your page is to make it engaging. If they go off and do not come back that is not because there was a link, it was because they did not feel the need to come back.

8. Keep it Informal and Conversational

This may be the most controversial rule on the list. There are many bloggers, often "real" writers, who will disagree with the contention that blogs need to stay informal and conversational. The goal is to no mimic professional journals or publications. The beginning of this book talked about the blog as a way to create a relationship with prospects and customers. Being too formal will not help with that goal.

The main reason for not going for a formal and very professional approach is that you set a high standard that you have to now live up to. When you make a mistake, have a typo, or cannot get a format just right, it will be very noticeable. If you start informal, you can stay informal and the need to spend time and money on perfection goes away.

You can also save on proofreading, which can be expensive. Instead of accepting the fact that you will have typos, misspellings, and mistakes, embrace it. Let your readers know up front that this is a conversation and a discussion.

Which goes to the second reason why this approach is recommended. You want to create a relationship with your audience. If you are too formal and not conversational, you ruin that friendliness. You are sharing your knowledge, not speaking down to people or worse, trying to sell them something. Greater loyalty will come from being a trusted, and friendly advisor.

So how do you keep it informal and conversational? What you do not want to do is force it. Throwing in slang and contractions to make it look like a conversation just does not work. Imagine yourself talking to a small group of people in a business setting and be yourself. If you use a lot of humor, and people laugh, then do that. If you like to make references to cheesy B-movies when talking about advanced electromechanical systems, then add that to your posts.

But if you are a more academic type of person and to the point, then do that. Just do not get too detailed or formal. Keep it loose, think tutoring session instead of lecture.

9. Use a Hierarchy Structure

One of the lost arts of journalistic writing that has been squashed by clickbait, and attempting to hook readers with outrage or salacious details, is the inverted pyramid. We want to organize information from most important to least important because people skim and they do not have the patience to look for what they want to really know.

If you are not familiar with the inverted pyramid, it usually looks something like this:

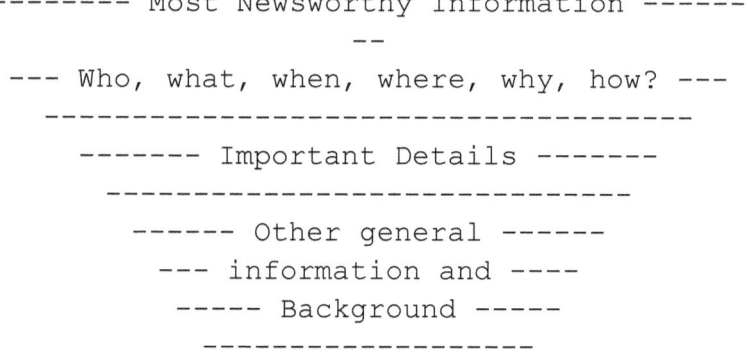

Use your favorite search engine to find more examples of how it all works.

The problem is that most of the time you are not going to be blogging about a news event. A hit and run at Main and Maple on Thursday night is very different from a post on the four new varieties of seedless watermelon you are offering. But it still applies.

Ask yourself what the: who, what, when, where, why, and how are for the information you want to convey. It may only be a what, or a how because there is no when or who. That is ok. The point is that your readers will want to know a few basic bits of information. Hopefully, the bits will be interesting enough for them to want some details followed by general and background information, often in the form of links.

To test this read the first one or two paragraphs of a post and ask yourself if you as a reader got the majority of what you need to know. If so, you are structuring your content correctly. If not, then try being more structured.

Although the big winner of this approach is your audience, it also helps in creating content. Most people struggle with sitting down and knocking out details. If you start with the key info, then list the details and background you think you will need you can then come back and fill things in. Much easier than starting at the hardest part.

It should be noted that there are key exceptions to this rule. One is when you are sharing a story. You are entertaining, and hopefully conveying information by taking your readers on a journey. You may want to hold the key information until the end, just as you never really know who did it in a mystery till the final pages. Just make sure your story is told well enough for people stick with it to the end.

You may be tempted to also lump a "how-to" article into the exceptions, but not really. The start of your article should contain that key information that people want, including a promise to give them a detailed step-by-step explanation of the "how." Then your important details section contains the steps.

10. Use Examples and Images

The final rule is one of the best aspects of blogging. Previous forms of writing required... well... lots of writing. Which is great if you are a writer. But if you were a writer you probably would be busy writing your third novel and not be interested in blogging for a business. With blogging, you can leverage the tried and true adage that a picture is worth a thousand words. And a good example is worth several hundred.

Remember that your goal is to educate and inform your audience, and it does not hurt to entertain them while you are at it. Unless you are an outstanding writer it is hard to do this with words only, so find ways to use examples and images to say what you want to say. If you find yourself struggling on a paragraph to explain something, time to go get an image. If you are still trying to explain some concept and you are in paragraph five, use an example instead.

Examples should be short and simplified. The best situation is where you have a real-world example that involves you or your company in some way. Or even better, with permission, a customer. But if you do not have any existing situations to use, just make something up.

Take watermellonmonger.com as an example of an imaginary example. It does not exist as of this writing, but it is a nice simple imaginary company that works as a great platform for examples. It is related to the topic at hand and is easy for people to understand.

As far as images go you should pick them based on two complementary criteria. They need to clearly convey an idea or concept, and they need to be appealing to the eye. They can be your own illustrations, screen captures, or camera pictures. Or you can use stock images. The options available are actually overwhelming, you just have to pick the right one.

Sometimes you may write something and there is really no need for an image to help convey what you wanted to say. That does not matter, add at least one or maybe two images. Just related stock images or a picture with some words on it. You need some graphics because today's world is a multi-media world, and your target will be turned off by nothing but text. So add some appropriate eye candy.

PART 3: BLOGGING TECHNIQUES

You know why you want to blog, you understand the rules, and maybe have set up some of your own. You can easily find a free blogging platform and start writing. But as you do so you will run into some problems. Hopefully, this part of the book will help you solve those problems and will assist you in being more productive as you blog your way to increased sales and profit.

1. How to get ideas

This is not true for everyone, but in general, the hardest thing to do is come up with ideas for posts. Everyone starts off with a list of post ideas and feel pretty good having a few extra ideas ready when you need them. Then time goes by, and that buffer gets smaller and next thing you know you are struggling to find content.

What follows are some simple techniques that can aid in keeping that list of ideas fresh and long.

Make it easy to capture ideas

Have a simple way to jot down ideas when you have them. A simple technique is to have a folder on a cloud-based file storage site that is available to your mobile, laptop, and desktop that you can throw ideas in. When one comes to you open up a word processor, enter the title and maybe a few sentences to expand on the idea or capture a key takeaway, then save that file in the shared directory. When it is time to write just open it up and start typing.

You may prefer to carry around a small leather-bound notebook. That way when you are in a coffee shop scribbling in it with a small pencil, people will think you are writing poetry. Or maybe you have a spreadsheet that is also on a shared cloud-based folder that you can list ideas in.

If you get an idea while out and about, say at a seminar or even a customer meeting. In those situations you cannot easily get to your directory. Instead, send yourself an email or a text. Then when you can open the email or text and put the idea into your standard place for collecting ideas.

Blog about what you learn

The best source for good content is to document something you have learned that is relevant to your target audience. Maybe you had to do a bunch of research to figure something out or you read an article that explained something to you. Perhaps you were just trying to do something, and it did not work, then you eventually figured it out. Anything that involves you gaining some sort of knowledge is a potential post idea.

Do not worry about it being too simple. If it took you five or ten minutes to figure something out, you could save someone time by explaining it to them in one minute. People want easy and they want things in easy to access chunks, so provide that to them.

Answer questions that customers ask

One way to make sure you are creating content that your customers are interested in is to keep track of the questions they ask and write articles about the most common questions. At the same time, interesting questions that are not so common will make a compelling post; because they are interesting.

This source of ideas has the added advantage of creating a connection with your customers and showing you as someone that listens and interacts with customers. So do not forget to point out that the idea came from a reader in your post.

Anything new is worth sharing – News

The Internet is full of information, but that does not mean your target audience gets all the news they are interested in. In fact, you can become their source for news on your industry. The nice thing about blogging about news is that you do not have to write most of the information, you simply have to link to an article that other people are writing. It does help to add your own perspective or opinion or maybe combine multiple sources for the news.

News posts are a great way to mix things up and some variety to your feed. Also, if you are stuck for an idea just read industry news and then blog about it. In as little as five minutes you will have content as well reinforcing yourself as a trusted expert and source of information.

Share a bit of information that got you excited or interested

If you run across any bit of information that captured your interest, that is in any way related to your industry, company, or community; it can be blog material. If it interests you there is a good chance it will interest the people who follow your blog.

Note that the topic does not have to be directly related to your industry, and "community" is a wide net. It can be your local community, a business community you belong to, or your profession.

But, do not fall into the trap of just putting in random stuff. Back in the day of newsletters it was common practice to include trivia or "fun facts" as filler… mostly to line up columns. We do not have to do that anymore and for a business blog, it will look like you are trying too hard.

Trends and changes in your industry

As a trusted advisor your readers will look to you to let them know not just what is going on in your shared area of interest, but also what you think about it. Trends and changes are different from news because they are not necessarily an event or some brand new thing.

Trends and changes are more subtle and reflect an honest observation that you have made based on your experience and knowledge. Maybe you notice that more of your suppliers are offering different colored watermelon. That is a trend. Figure out why and what it means and then blog about it. Are consumers excited about it? Does it remind you of a trend in the past?

If you can show your knowledge and expertise while sharing useful information you have hit a blogging home run.

What is going on at your company

There are a lot of advantages to sharing information about your company. The most obvious advantage is that you can use it to market what you are doing. New services or products, a new business line, and hopefully your continued and accelerating success are all things worth sharing that your audience cares about.

In most cases, it is hard to get local or industry press to cover what you are up to, and fewer people read such publications anyway, so use your blog to share information you wish they were reporting on about you. But do not overdo it. You do not want your blog to turn into a brochure or one big long press release. Share what is new or interesting but add something special to it. Share why the changes are important or maybe thank your customers for helping you get where you are.

The other reason why you should share what is going on at your place of business is that people who are customers, or potential customers, are part of a community that you are building around your company. Because of this, they want to know what is going on inside. The more you involve them in the "thing" that is your business, the more loyalty and attraction they will have for your products and services.

The last reason for talking about your company is that, and it may not be nice to say, your website may be stagnant and unattractive to search engines. But your blog, because you publish useful information often, is alive and well and well-liked by the algorithms in the cloud. If you talk about what you do in your blog the odds of a search engine finding on a more active portion of your web presence, and then promoting it, are higher. This leads to more leads and more business.

Suggestions from other people

Friends, family, co-workers, and readers are the best sources of ideas. If you let people know you are blogging and that you are open to suggestions they will naturally make recommendations. People you know may not write or want to write, but they think of good topics.

Asking for suggestions does present a problem. What do you do when they come up with a bad idea? If you are a stronger person, you let them know it is not a good fit. If you are a coward, you say you put it on your list, but it has not bubbled to the top yet.

Your opinion (and courting controversy)

Even though a blog is a great place to share your deeply held convictions that irrigation of watermelon through drip watering is tantamount to using the blood of new sacrificed puppies as fertilizer, it is probably not a good idea. If you hold a strong opinion on something there will be others who hold the exact opposite opinion, and they will get mad about it. In general courting controversy is not a good idea.

Or... maybe it is a good idea. One of the goals of a business blog is to attract attention, and nothing gets attention like controversy. But, and it is a big but, it may be the wrong type of attention. The primary goal is to increase business and if you invite passion you may also invite anger, anger towards you and your company. A good middle ground is to go ahead and share your opinion, but not an opinion that can generate anger. Watch how you present the opinion and include justification for your point of view. At the same time, you need to stay away from inflammatory additions. For our example, point out the reasons why you do not like drip irrigation for watermelon, but try to avoid comparisons to infant canine butchery.

You can express your opinion on a lot of things without being controversial. When you do so, make sure you let people know it is just an opinion and not fact. Then invite your readers to share their opinion. It is another opportunity to build a relationship and let them feel a part of what you are doing.

If you do feel the need to share something controversial that is fine. Just make sure it is something you care enough about to risk business for. Maybe you are a strong proponent of genetically modified watermelons Maybe you are a foe. Either way, people tend to be very emotional about GMO's. So be willing to take a stand and deal with the consequences. It will get you readers, and it may also lose customers.

2. The Goal, Outline, Story Technique

If you are a natural writer, the kind of person that can come up with an idea and just knock out 500 to 1,000 with no problem, skip this section. You do not need help, and your skills bother the rest of us. Go write something and then come back and read the next session.

OK, now that the rest of us are alone, we need to be honest. It takes a lot of focus and some special skills to sit down and crank out a post. That blank page, or even a page with a good title, can be terrifying. Everyone has their tricks and methods to make it easier. One process that many find useful consists of breaking the task into three steps: define the goal, create an outline, and then tell a story by filling in the outline.

Before I go over each step, it is important to note that this process only works for certain types of writing. If you are doing a how-to or a short post that references something else, this does not really help. But if you are sharing a lot of information, over 400 words or show, it is very helpful.

Define the Goal

This book stresses the importance of creating goals for a reason. If you know what you want to achieve with a piece it makes writing the piece a lot easier. That is because you have to make decisions throughout the process and you need to keep things short and to the point. Knowing a goal helps with making those decisions and staying brief.

The section in the introduction on goals was about overall goals for your blog. You want to make sure that each post addresses those goals. Now it is time to think about the specific goals of an individual post. Note that you need one goal, but it is OK to have two or three less important goals.

What do you want to accomplish with your post? Is it to introduce a new service or product? Is it to build customer loyalty through entertainment? It may be to drive people to an event. What the goal does not matter as much as deciding on what you want to do and writing it down.

A good technique is to write the goal at the top of your document, and then enter your prose above it. Get rid of that blank page right away. Use a weird font so you notice it and remember to remove it before you upload it. "Convince my less intelligent customers that sour watermelon is actually good for you so I can move this inventory" at the bottom of a post will not help sales. But having it there while you are writing really helps.

As an example, let's start with the idea of writing an article on the different ways to cut a watermelon. The goal is to get people excited about doing something fun and different with watermelon and ordering one from our website. Since this imaginary company also sells devices for cutting watermelon, a secondary goal is to drive sales of those.

Create an Outline

Outlines are a wonderful thing for quickly building up content without having to slug through mounds of words. It allows you to start at a very high level and then add detail, then more detail, then have everything you need to start writing.

In general, all outlines for a blog post should have a title, an introduction, the main section, and a conclusion. At the same time, the story can and should follow the structure of the inverted pyramid. Start with that. Now your page is even less blank. If someone walks behind you, they will see something on your screen. Progress has been made.

The next step is up to you because you have to start filling in details. You can stay at a high level and work your way through every level, then add details to everything. Or you can pick one area and dig all the way down moving to the next area when you have enough. Whatever works. And do not be afraid of jumping around. While discussing one topic you may think of something for the introduction – stop and add it. The same goes for when you start writing the post. If something pops into your head that you want to make sure you capture, stick it in the outline so you do not forget. Keeping it at the bottom of your document makes it easy. Some of the best ideas come to you while you are writing.

The outline does not have to be complete nor will you follow it exactly. It is a tool for your writing and nothing more. Over time you will figure out how to best use it for the way you work.

Staying with our example, an outline for our cutting post might look like this:

1) Title
    a) Add fun to your snacks with eight different ways to cut your watermelon
2) Introduction
    a) Great thing about watermelon is that it can be cut into all sorts of shapes
    b) This is fun to do
    c) A way to make your fruit fancy
    d) Do not be afraid, start with simple ways and work your way to more complicated
3) Main Article
    a) Eight Shapes

  i) Sticks
   (1) Easy to eat
   (2) Kids can do this
  ii) Wedges
   (1) Classic but hard to eat
  iii) Rounds
   (1) Stackable
   (2) Mozzarella!
  iv) Triangles
   (1) Kids love this shape for easy eating
  v) Cookie Cutters
  vi) Circles
  vii) Balls
  viii) Cubes
  ix) Random
 b) Mix it up for fun
 c) Each kid can cut a shape
 d) Use the rind as a bowl
 e) Once mastered, this can really jazz up your presentation.
 f) Tools
  i) Good sharp knife is needed
  ii) Baller
  iii) Cookie cutters
  iv) Curved knife
 g) Conclusion
 h) Remind them that they can do it and its fun
 i) Try your own ideas, experiment
 j) Call to Action - buy from us!

Write the Story

It can no longer be put off. It's time to make paragraphs. For people not used to writing the important thing to keep in mind is that you are telling a story. Simply listing facts or observations is boring and no one will read it.

A story is defined as "a narrative, either true or fictitious, in prose or verse, designed to interest, amuse, or instruct the hearer or reader; tale." It is not a random pile of facts and information. Your readers expect a beginning, a middle, and an end. But, within the middle and maybe the introduction, try and use the inverted pyramid.

How to write a story is beyond the scope of this book. But some basics can help.

One of the most important is to remember that your paragraphs need to be a single idea. Maybe it's one item in your outline per paragraph. A common mistake in business blogs is the never-ending paragraph. New-line characters cost nothing, use them.

A related technique is to connect the thoughts from one paragraph to another. An abrupt transition hurts. Take this paragraph. If could have started it with "Another technique..." or "The next technique to remember..." All of those work. If it had started with "Connect the thoughts from one paragraph to another" it would have been too abrupt.

> Note: A section heading of some kind is a great way to do an abrupt transition.

After you have thought about paragraphs (see how that statement relates back...) you need to focus on your sentences. Everyone's writing style varies. You can be bold like Hemingway. Punch your thoughts out. Writing is tough work and it takes a tough mind to do it.

Or, if it is more fitting to your own personal style, the method, and technique that you have developed over time; you may find that it is better, perhaps more comfortable, to weave your narrative into a Dickensian tapestry of words and phrases connected with ephemeral commas that allow your thoughts to skip from point to point like a well-tossed stone, skipping across a glass-smooth lake on a crisp spring morning, the ripples disturbing the perfect reflection of the snow-clad mountains in the distance.

Long winded or abrupt, pick a style and stick with it. But within that style do try and vary your sentence structure. Shake up word order, use a comma now and then. Do not be afraid of a hyphen – they can be useful to make a strong point.

The last bit of advice for creating a story is to keep it interesting. Humor, asides, silly references, and a well-placed image can help your narrative along.

Remember your outline – use it. Even if your fingers are flying stop at some point and review the outline. The same goes for your goal or goals. When you finish a paragraph, or maybe when you are in the middle of it, ask yourself if it is addressing the goal. Remove or reword paragraphs that drift from your goal.

And when you are done, edit. The secret of most good writers is that they spend more time editing than they do writing. As a blogger for a business who is trying to minimize cost, you do not have time for that. But you need to do at least one edit. That is where a good post turns into a great one.

3. Writing a "How-To"

One of the best uses of a business related blog is a "How-To." This is an article where you show your readers how to do something. It is not a full tutorial or training class. It is also not a list of ideas on how people can use your product or service. It is a step-by-step description leading the reader through the process of doing something.

The "How-To" is a staple of the IT and software world. Explaining how to better use the products you make or sell fits right into almost all the reasons why you are doing a business blog. Even if you are not in tech, there may be plenty of opportunities to share a "How-To" and give value to your existing and potential customers, build loyalty with them, and increase your reputation as a domain expert.

In the example from the previous section, we made up an imaginary blog about different ideas on cutting up watermelon. Multiple follow-on "How-To" posts would be step-by-step instructions on how to do each of the cutting options mentioned.

The format of a "How-To" should be fairly simple: an introduction with some background, a numbered list of steps with details and images to explain each step, and a conclusion. The conclusion sums things up, points to additional or related information, and makes some sort of call to action. Use numbered headers and if it makes sense, an image for each stop.

Now you may be asking yourself, "Isn't a video better and easier?" Yes. If a video makes sense do a video instead. Keep the introduction and conclusion, but replace the written steps including pictures with an embedded video. It's not a bad idea to also list the steps in the introduction to the video for search engines to find.

A good process for writing "How-To" posts is to do the thing once, do the thing again taking notes as you go, write your post, and finally do the thing following the post and making corrections as you go. The last step is critical in making your instructions good. If possible have a co-worker or trusted customer go through the instructions and take notes while you watch them.

Another tip is to make sure you find that balance between conciseness and details. If you include everything, people will get overwhelmed and not read your post. But if you do not include enough details then someone trying to use your "How-to" may be unsuccessful, and that is bad. No impression is better than a negative impression.

If you have not created a "How-To" before or you have not used many, you should start with some very simple tasks. It is easy to assume that you readers know how to do the simple things in your industry. But that is not true. Some of the most popular posts written are "How-To" articles on basic tasks. Remember, you are probably an expert. Your average audience member may not be an expert, or they may just want the confidence of a well-written blog article to get started doing the thing you want to help them get better at doing.

4. Sharing News

A fantastic type of content in a business blog, and often the easiest to create, is content that shares some sort of news. These are great because you do not have to do a lot of research, document a process, or come up with an interesting narrative. You just need to report the news interestingly and add some insight to show your value as a trusted advisor. In fact, some companies just have someone, often an intern, assigned to reading the news and tagging articles that might fit their blog.

Readers look to trusted advisors to help them understand why things are important, to summarize and simplify, and to relate the news to their situation. If you can do one or more of those things, you will have achieved many of the goals of business blogging.

A good place to start with sharing news is figuring out what your spin is on the news. It should at least be that your audience cares about the topic being discussed. If that interest is all there is, let them know you found something they might be interested in. Share the news, provide a link, and then stop.

Most of the time there is an opportunity to add more value, and you should take advantage of it. A common characteristic to look for is news that can be used by your audience to their advantage. If you are a business-to-business company, perhaps the news can help your business customer improve their profit or get to market before someone else. If you sell to consumers then perhaps it improves their quality of life, or it can save them money.

Your blog post should not only share the news. It is also very important for you to explain what the advantages to or impact on your readers are. Sharing a story about a new strain of watermelon that has been shown to reduce cholesterol is great on its own, but it will not improve your business much unless you also highlight the cholesterol-lowering benefits and point it out as an advantage.

Explaining and simplifying is another approach you can take to sharing news. The primary news source may be too technical, or the story may be too complex. If you can simplify it or make the news understandable, you have created value and once again shown yourself to be a trusted advisor.

As far as structure goes, that really depends on the news and how good the outside source is. If you are sharing information from an actual news source, a real journalist created it, then just linking to that story is enough. If the source does not have all of the information it should, you need to include your version of the news. Overall, you should follow your normal structure.

Introduce the story with some sort of a pull - why is it important to a reader or why you found it interesting. Then share the story including links. Follow that with your observation and analysis. You should then end the post with some call to action: links for more information on your site, or a statement saying that they should call or email if they want to talk about this further or understand better how it impacts them directly.

5. Blogging about Events: Invites, and Recaps

Events of various kinds have proven over time to be one of the best tools for sales and marketing, especially for business-to-business. Conferences, seminars, grand openings, and webinars provide opportunities to connect with people and share information live. And because they are live you get better interaction and create stronger ties.

These same characteristics make them good subject matter for blogs. You can advertise an event to drive attendance and show people that you do events. It also indicates what your company shares and cares about. After the event you can talk about what happened, reinforce the messaging from the event, and give some of what you communicated to people who could not make it. All good stuff for a small investment of time.

A blog is a great place to share invitations even if it does not really drive that much attendance. Your regular readers will see the event that is coming and hopefully attend. The number of people you want to reach who regularly read the blog is probably not as much as you would like. Email invitations and social media do a better job of getting people to show up. The real benefit of blogging your invitations is that after the fact, people know you held the event. It will show up in search engines and will be found by people just browsing your content. This again shows your readers what you care about and how you support the community around you.

The other way to get blogging benefit from events is doing a recap. This is where you talk about the events your company was part of. This can be activities you hosted or other events that you attended.

It is a fantastic way to leverage your participation in a trade show or other industry-specific events.

You should of course post to social media while you are at an event. Take lots of pictures beyond what you need for social media though, especially of customers and partners, so that when you do your recap, you can include them in your story. People like to see themselves or people like them.

Posts about an event should not be any different from any other post. They need to be interesting, share something of value, and draw your customers in with some call to action. The best is if you learned something worth sharing or if you presented content that your readers might be interested in. Include either in your story.

For seminars and similar types of presentations, it is great to include the slides in the post. If you recorded the event then you can share a link to that recording. In most cases you will want to make people register to view a recording. And any day you can add an email to your distribution list is a good day for marketing.

6. Executing on Funny or Silly Posts

One of the best ways to entertain and attract customers is through humor. People like to laugh, and it makes them feel good which certainly is something positive to associate with your brand. Along the same line, a little bit of silliness also helps create a less formal connection to your readership, making them part of an inner circle that is in on the joke. It can also help soften what may be a harsh corporate impression of your company, or spice up a boring industry or product offering.

The reality is that when people laugh their brain gets a dose of endorphins, which is a feel-good chemical. Having that associated with your brand can have a very powerful subconscious effect. And one of the nice things about blogging is that it is informal and a casual way of communicating with your market, the perfect place to let your hair down a little and have some fun.

So, does this imply that you should follow the old adage of start your speech with a joke to loosen up the audience? "I just flew in from Detroit, and boy are my arms tired!" Um…. No.

First off, you need to make sure that humor or silliness fits your brand. If you are a funeral home – not a good fit. If you work for a very large company it may fit, but it is so hard to control, and once the genie is out of the bottle you cannot keep it in. It's probably better to stay away.

If these situations do not apply and you feel humor can help your marketing, there is a second thing to consider.

It is really hard to be funny!

Especially when you are trying to be funny. And being silly can come off as stupid instead of casual and fun. So tread lightly. Do not go down the road of humor unless you have thick skin, you can look at your content objectively, and you want to be more casual with your brand.

Now that all the warning signs are out of the way it is time to get serious about not being serious. Here are some key lessons on humor in blogs... some of which were learned the hard way:

Do not try too hard

The easiest way to kill a joke is to look like you are telling a joke. If you have ever gone to an open mic night at a comedy club you will see this first hand. Humor needs to be natural and maybe even a bit of a surprise.

Everyone has their own personal way of being funny. Maybe you are sarcastic or you like to point out absurdities. Go with that. Use the humor you are most comfortable with and your effort will look natural for a simple reason – it is natural.

A good way to avoid looking like you are trying too hard is to only sprinkle in humor. Do not try and make an entire post funny or silly. It is good to start or finish with some funny. End and begin with a smile. Or take a break in the middle of something serious or a bit boring. Think of it as a comedy break.

The last thing you want to do is plan out a joke or funny thing. If it does not flow on its own, leave it alone.

Let them know you are trying to be funny

Unless your blog has a reputation for humor, if you are throwing a small bit of funny in, or the whole post is obviously a fun piece, then you need to make sure it is obvious that you are trying to be funny. You do not want your readers to be confused. If they are not expecting humor or silliness, they may get a feeling of unease because the words they are reading do not line up with their expectations. This releases brain chemicals you do not want to be associated with your brand.

Simply stating "this is a funny post" at the start violates the "do not try too hard" rule. A better way to make it obvious is to use a visual that lets people know right away you are not trying to be serious. Because people will look at the images before they read, you can use that as a clue. Some humor in the title does the same thing.

Another way to point it out is to transition from humor to serious with a statement basically saying "that was fun, but let's get serious now" in a way that flows well.

Do not offend

Some of the best humor pokes fun at things, especially groups of people. Save that for the stand-up routine and do not put it in a blog.

This seems obvious but needs to be stated clearly: Do not do anything that might alienate any of your audience.

It can be done well, but in most cases it can backfire because social networks allow a small number of people a big voice. You may publish something that 99% of your readers find funny but that

1% that gets offended can go on Twitter to express outrage. The outrage starts a troll war and the next thing you know your brand is the lead story on the news about corporate "tone-deafness" to some cause or group.

In most cases, the best thing you can do is ask yourself: are you funny or are you making fun of something or someone? Avoid making fun of things. If the joke is at the expense of someone or something else, it is best to just not use it.

As an example, with watermelonmonger.com an article making fun of people who like to cut up their watermelon into equally sized perfect cubes might be hilarious. The downside is you are making fun of people who like to do that, and they may suffer from Obsessive Compulsive Disorder. They get mad, and the International OCD Foundation hears about it and starts a boycott of your business. A very thorough and well-organized boycott, where every detail is worked out and documented in color coded notebooks.

Instead, maybe tell a story about wanting to cut an entire watermelon into perfect cubes and how proud you were to finally do it after three attempts. Talk about how bad your bad attempts were and maybe how your family looked at you strangely. If told right this is relatable, funny, and engaging without making someone or something the butt of the joke.

You are better off just avoiding anything that might be offensive. Language, topics, groups, and causes. There are plenty of other things to build humor around.

Make references that your readership will get

A tried and true way to get humor is to slide in references that are inside jokes or that remind people of something. It shows that you are aware and brings your readers into an "inner circle" that creates a tighter connection to you and your brand. It is also a way to be funny without being funny. Instead of saying something humorous you just point to something that is.

This is great, except when your readership does not get it. Talking about taking a trip and bringing an intern along as a "red shirt" and how they did not make it back to the office, will crack up nerds between the age of 30 and 60. But anyone else will not get it or think you are talking about a college athlete that sat out their freshman year. Did you get it? If yes you probably chuckled, and you are a nerd. If not, type 'red shirt away team" into your favorite search engine and it will explain why this is the perfect inside reference for middle-aged nerds.

What this hopefully shows is that using a reference is only funny if enough of your readers get it. If they do, it is great. But if they do not they are just confused and may have negative feelings about you and your brand.

Where this is especially true is when you are trying to reach an international or multicultural audience. References that work in your country or your culture may not just go over the heads, they may actually offend.

So the best policy is to just avoid references unless you feel you really know your audience and understand what they will follow.

Self-deprecating humor backfires for blog posts

A go-to standby in most situations is self-deprecating jokes. But not necessarily on a blog. Unlike in social situations or with friends, the goal of a blog is not to disarm people by making fun of yourself. You are trying to build your brand and create a positive impression. Poking fun at yourself, your products, or your brand does not reinforce positive impressions.

Worse, you are giving ammunition to your competitors. What started as funny can turn into a weapon against you. Even though it can be a great way to break the ice and even garner empathy that is not what you want to achieve in a business blog.

Some good tools: Parody, Puns, and Pop Culture

Enough of what does not work. What does work, again and again, is: parody, puns, and pop culture references. The three P's of safe humor.

Parody is the humorously exaggerated imitation of something else. Usually, something that a lot of people know and understand. It is a way to grab attention and create a positive emotional response that makes you and your brand look connected and smart.

Puns are one of those things that people love to groan about. A good pun is almost painful, but it is also smart and funny. As long as you think your readers will get it, pun away. And it is not a bad idea to make sure they know you are attempting to be punny by saying "pun intended" or something like that.

The great thing about pop culture references is that you are referencing something that is popular. It is an easy and effective way to bring your readers into your circle, or for you to join theirs. There is something bonding about remembering and laughing at a common cultural touchstone.

Have a humor checker

Funny is subjective. Just as you should have someone check for grammar and typos, you need to have someone check your humor. They need to make sure your content is not only funny but that it does not offend anyone or go too far.

Make sure you pick someone who may not share your ethnic, generational, and cultural background. Remember, this is a check on you, so you need someone who can look at things differently. And then, this is the hard part, make sure you do not take their observations personally. If they say "it's not funny," "it is offensive," or "I do not get it" try not to push back. Except it and adjust.

Remember to still deliver good content

Sometimes it is easy to get wrapped up in humor and forget that the goal of your blog post is not to be funny. You are using humor to enhance your post, not as the point of the post. So keep in mind all the other rules and suggestions about blogging and make sure you do not leave them out.

7. Getting Others to Create Content

One of the most difficult tasks in blogging for your business is getting other people in your organization to create content. You may have a source, maybe it's you, that likes to write, and they do a good job. The problem is that in most cases you need multiple voices to have breadth and depth of content. In an ideal world you send an email out every once in a while to your organization asking for posts and you receive a steady, high-quality stream from multiple people. They have read this book, are good about adhering to your blogging goals, and they never have typos.

Back in the real world; we have to find ways to find to encourage content creators.

Every organization is different so you will have to take different approaches and maybe change them over time to keep that content coming. There are generally three reasons why people do not want to contribute:

1) *They just are not good at it.*
   That is OK. Recognize it and move on, everyone will be better off.

2) *They do not have time.*
   If what they have to offer your blog is of high value and the blog is having an impact, it is time to talk with management and make contributing part of their job. Change their priorities and set aside enough time for them to get some posts out on a regular basis.

3) *Fear.*
   This is the most common problem. They fear that their writing will not be good enough, it is not complete

enough, or that people will laugh at them or troll them. For some people, this is just like public speaking because it exposes them and makes them vulnerable. The best solution in this situation is to ease them in. Start small and simple and get the ball rolling. Over time have them do more and more till they get the confidence to be a regular participant in your company's online marketing.

So how do you get them to start working? The first thing you can do is seek out and encourage those who like to write and are good at it. This can start by seeking and finding good internal content. Maybe an employee gave a great presentation or sent out an email that was well written and informative. Approach them and let them know that you liked it and that it would be great content for the company blog.

Sharing good examples with the organization or just those you want to encourage can really help to get people over any fear they have. It might even spark some competition. When you share the example, just as in a blog post, make sure you point out why it is a good example and have a call to action.

Here is an example of what that could look like:

> "Big thanks to Susan for this great write-up on detecting ripeness from color. It is short, has great pictures, and gets people thinking about enjoying a watermelon. She told me it only took her about an hour to put together. If you have anything you want to share with our customers, shoot me an email or stop by my cube and let's work out a post."

If your company offers technical or customer support of any kind, that team can be a great source for your blog. The employees that provide support are providing content to customers all day, every day. It does not take much to convert that into a stream of posts. Start by simply making them aware of the opportunity.

Let them know that you need content and they should email you when they get off a call or close out a support ticket and they shared something that others might find useful. You can then give them feedback and ask for a post of some kind. Maybe a regular visit to wherever they sit and some casual conversation will pop out some posts.

Another way to motivate people is to give them a copy of this book. Or maybe you can do an internal seminar or write an email sharing some key things you have learned from this book. Knowing that there is a resource to help them through the process can be very helpful.

In most cases just asking and encouraging is very effective. In some cases, you just have to force it and get management to mandate that content must be contributed to the blog. This can be a quota per employees in a certain area or by group in the company. In a technical organization with a technical support group, one post per quarter per support engineer for a smaller group and one per year for a big one is not a bad requirement.

Lastly, someone may have to step up and serve as editor and/or writer. Many people have great information to share, but they just cannot write. All the coaxing in the world will not change that. What does work is getting the important part, the information, out of them and packaging it as a post yourself.

With technical people, getting them to make a PowerPoint presentation works well. In many cases they already have content in a slide deck. You can use it directly adding an introduction and call to action. Or you can read the slides and turn it into a written story.

Another great method is to interview them and write a story. Professional content creators do this all the time. Get the expert to share their information by asking questions then turn around and write what you learned. It is a great idea to even list the employee as the author to encourage them to provide more. There are worse things than being a ghostwriter on a company blog. Not having enough content for your blog being one of them

PART 4: THE MECHANICS OF BLOGGING

Most of this book has focused on the creation of content, but at some point you have to post it on your blog. That is where you need to pay attention to efficiently getting your hard work out there and learn the tools and techniques needed to present your content to the world. As with any endeavor, tasks are much easier when you use the right tools. The good news is that most of what you need is free, affordable, or something you should already have. You just need to pick which you will use and learn them.

When picking your tools make sure you go with something that is stable, will be around for a while, is easy to use, and is simple. Remember, we want to be efficient and quick so everything does not have to be perfect.

Technique is really about quickly and efficiently getting your content in a form that displays well to readers. How you set up your blogging site is critical here because most of the layout process is automatically handled by your blogging platform. Once you set it up, you do not have to worry about it again.

1. Blogging Platforms

This is your most important decision. A blogging platform is a piece of software that runs on a computer with a web server on it. The web server is how browsers connect to the computer and request content. To the user, the blogging platform presents your content in an organized way to the web server so that readers can read it. For the blogger, it provides a way to create, organize, publish, edit, and monitor your content. It also formats everything for you, creating the look and feel of your blog.

As of the writing of this book, there really is only one platform that dominates in this space: WordPress. The good news is that the software is free because it is still open source. But you need to either host it yourself or pay a hosting service. You will also want to put it under your company's domain:

```
blog.watermelonmonger.com
```

or

```
www.watermelonmonger.com/blog
```

The domain registration has an annual fee associated with it, but your company probably already have a domain name. The domain and hosting are just not that big of an investment, it is surprisingly the least expensive part of doing a business blog. In fact, most of the companies that sell domain names also offer packages with web hosting that include everything you need to do a blog set up and ready to go with technical support.

The first place to start in deciding on a platform, or more likely where to host your WordPress, is with your IT team. Specifically, whoever is responsible for hosting your website. Odds are they already have a blogging platform installed, or if you are hosted in the cloud, your provider has a platform available as part of your package. Go with whatever you have, do not make things more complicated. The key is to get started and get content out there. If you are successful, you can get a better platform.

What do you do if IT does not already have a solution for you? If you are a technically oriented company with a good IT team, then download WordPress and install it on your website. This makes it free and you control everything. However, nothing is completely free because you are now responsible for backups, updates, and dealing with any problems.

If this causes you to go into full panic mode, then get out your favorite search engine and look up WordPress hosting. Look around and just pick one. There are a lot of options including some blog posts ranking hosting sites. The most important thing here is that you go with someone established with good customer service. WordPress is fairly easy to use, but if you are not technical you will want to be able to call someone who will walk you through the steps. If you are comfortable configuring your own site, then you can save some money each month.

Once you have made your choice work with IT to get a URL pointing to your site and then get started. The key to getting up and running fast is using templates and styles, covered in the next session. Take your time in these early days on your blog to get to know the tools for your site. Go online and find videos and articles with basic how-to's and tutorials. You may even want to play with your site for a few weeks before you launch it. Make a bunch of test posts and play around, then just delete it all and start when you are ready to go live.

But have no fear, if you do nothing but take the defaults and just start posting, you will be way ahead of your competitors who do not have a blog or are still worrying over making it perfect.

Note: Now that you are getting down into the weeds of setting stuff up, do not lose sight of the most important message in this book: publish useful content often.

2. Templates and Styles

A big advantage of the way that blogging sites work is that they use predefined templates and styles to handle all the details about what your pages look like, what fonts are used, and how pictures are displayed. Everything from backgrounds to the color of hyperlinks is set up and consistent across the site. Once these options are set all you have to do is add content.

The only decision needed from you is picking that template. The best option is doing as little as possible. Go with a simple, easy to read format. You may be tempted to pick something sophisticated and fancy so your posts will stand out. Do not fall for it! It is a trap! Go for a white background and use your corporate color scheme to highlight not to dominate the look and feel.

Most sites use some sort of a header as an anchor for each page of content. This is where you may want to consult any graphic artists you have available. Work with them to pick a compelling heading that conveys your brand and is consistent with your website and any printed material you may have. If you do not have that type of resource use a simple image or go with your logo on a plain background. Remember that logo and color are how you reinforce your brand. Anything more may not even be noticed.

It is easy to get wrapped up in your own bubble when picking templates, so one suggestion is that you copy and paste some random content from another blog into your blogging site to get three or four posts to play with. Then try different templates and show them to other people. Not just within your company, go outside to friends and family or perhaps a few trusted customers. Style is very subjective and you will rarely get a consensus. But if something is not working you will get feedback on that. The goal here is to avoid something that is bad, not to find the perfect look and feel.

For most people the default templates and style sheets work. You can certainly do more if you want, but it is not going to drastically change your number of readers.

If you do not know what an XML or CSS file is, then stop reading and go to the next session.

Now we can get deep and dirty into formatting. If you know your way around cascading style sheets, you can change almost anything. Read the help on your blogging software about where the files are and how to edit them. As always, do not change the defaults, make copies and edit those.

Do not make any large changes, the templates and style sheets that come with them tend to be fairly well done and balanced. Changing a font or a color may throw off the balance of the composition. Also, be aware that the template and stylesheet may have a mobile and desktop version, change both if needed.

You may want to add some of your own classes for some standard objects that you want to format different than the defaults. An example is using a class for <img>'s that puts a border around an image. This is useful when you have a white background and the image does too, so it bleads into the page. A thin border sets it apart. If this paragraph makes no sense to you, then just use the defaults. Move along. Nothing to see here.

3. The Built-in Editor

Most blogging sites come with good enough editors to create your content. The one that comes inside WordPress is very good and for most users, is the right way to create and format your content. Remember that our goal is to get good content up quick, so we do not want or need lots of bells and whistles for formatting.

These editors are very basic when compared to a word processor, but close enough to where there is no learning curve. Since most of your content is going to be text and images you need to focus on those two things. Text is easy, just type and do not play around with fonts and text decoration.

Make sure spell check is turned on. Even if you are a good speller, it will find some typos. The other tool you need to get good with is the one that you use to create hyperlinks. In most cases you highlight the text you want to be a link, click the link icon, and then enter the URL you want to send the user to. You can also click on the more or settings icon in the link dialog. This will bring up another dialog where you can do things like telling the system to open the link in a new tab and change the text that is displayed for the link. You can also put in a search term to jump to (anchor) within your article. More on that in the section on HTML.

And, shockingly, that is about it. For most posts you will insert images or maybe a video. If you find yourself wanting to do more, then maybe you are trying to do too much. Some more advanced editing topics are covered in this book but do remember that the goal in business blogging is to minimize the investment and just get the content out there. If you are trying to embed a javascript to animate a frame containing dynamic content, you have missed the point, unless you are writing a blog post about using java to animate dynamic content.

4. Using Word Processors

The final version of your post should be edited with the editor built into your blogging software. But for many people logging in and working in that environment adds additional effort and learning. This is especially true if you are trying to get other people in your company to provide content. In most cases, it is easier to create the content in a word processor that you know well, then paste it into the blog editor when it is all done. Getting your content writers to log into the blogging tool is another step that keeps them from getting your content. Make it easy, have them write in a word processor.

The key to doing this successfully is to ignore all the bells and whistles in the word processor. Use the default formatting and insert images without formatting. This is because that formatting probably will not translate into proper formatting in your blog and you will need to spend a lot of time cleaning things up.

The recommended approach is to keep things plain and simple, then copy and paste the text as text into your editor. Some editors have a "paste from Microsoft Word" that cleans up a lot of incompatible formatting, but you are often better off just pasting as text.

If the word processor document had images, go to the word processor and right-mouse-button on each image and save it to disk, and give it a name. Assigning a good name is very important because search engines will read that name. If you just copy and paste the images, they will be assigned random text strings for names. Take the time to add a descriptive file name, with an underscore (_) or dash (-) for spaces. Also, give it a figure number, say F01, F02, F03.

As an example, if you want to save three pictures of three different colors of watermelon, you would call them something like:

```
water-melon-colors-red-f01.jpg
water-melon-colors-green-f02.jpg
water-melon-colors-yellow-f03.jpg
```

Now when someone searches for green watermelon images, your site has a good chance of showing up. Once you have saved them with good names, use the built-in editor's tool to insert the images in the proper place.

The other thing that is good about this paste-from-a-word-processor approach is that it forces you to read and edit the content. Go through it to format and check one last time for grammar and any areas that need a final tweak.

5. HTML Editing

One of the beauties of blogging is that you can create high-quality readable content without knowing the page layout language that web browser read and interpret: HTML. The HyperText Markup Language is the commonly agreed upon way to store information you want people to view through a web browser. What web browsers actually do is go to a web server (the address you put in at the top) and say "give me HTML" then take that HTML and render it as a page. There is a bit more to it (scripts and embedded style sheets) but that is basically what is happening.

So blogging software allows you to supply text and embedded media, and it handles most of the HTML to get it formatted the right way. But if you want to have some control over the look and feel, you need to provide more than text, you have to add some of your own HTML.

If you know HTML, even basic, you are good. Use a search engine to refresh yourself on anything you do not remember. If HTML is a mystery to you, there are a few basic things you need to know covered below.

The way HTML works is you enclose text or the address of media inside tags to tell the browser what to do with the stuff inside the tabs. A tag is a keyword and some modifiers stuck inside a less than and greater-than <, > signs. The start tag is <keyword> and the end tag is </keyword>. So if you want to make something bold, you put it in between the tag <strong> and </strong>. As an example:

```
This is an example of <strong>bold text</strong> in HTML
```

Renders as:

> This is an example of **bold text** in HTML.

There are hundreds of HTML tags, and many of them are handled by your built-in blogging editor. To save time and be efficient, you should know the basics to modify your posts or maybe understand why they do not look right when something goes wrong.

To view and edit the HTML for your posts your editor should have a button or a tab that says "text" or "HTML."

Here are the tags that anyone who is editing blog content should know about:

<h1><h2><h3> - Headings

The most important tags for a blog are the heading tags: <h1><h2><h3>. That is because search engines look for headings and because it gives your posts a consistent look a feel when it comes to headings. <h1> should be a major heading, <h2> the next level, and <h3> minor headings. You can go to <h6> but you should not, that is just too much formatting and is annoying. Your editor probably has a way to select text and assign these headers automatically.

<p> - Paragraph

Most of your text blog posts will be paragraphs. In most blogging systems you do not need to mark paragraphs as such, they are rendered automatically. But to be sure, you can use <p>text</p> to control the start and stop of a paragraph.

<pre> - Preformatted Text

If you are doing a technical blog and you want to show script of code, use the <pre>code</pre> tag to display the text you want to set apart. It will use a fixed width font, and it is one of the rare places in HTML where multiple spaces and tabs are not removed. This is critical for showing indented code.

As an example the following HTML:

```
<p>Type   the   following   command   into   the   command
line:</p>
<pre>ls -la</pre>
<p>Will  give  a  detailed  list  of  the  files  in  the
current directory</p>
```

Look like:

> Type the following command into the command line:
>
> ```
>     ls -la
> ```
>
> Will give a detailed list of the files in the current directory

<blockquote> - Quotation

If you want to set a block of text apart to stand out, especially a quote, then use the <blockquote> tags around the text. Not only does it look better but search engines like it.

 - Line Break

Most of the time if you put a line break into your text in the text editor, it will show up on your blog post as a new line. But if you need to control it explicitly use <br> for a line break that is not necessarily the start of a new paragraph.

<hr> - Horizontal Line

It may be considered a little old-fashioned, but sometimes it is nice to have a simple horizontal line in your post to separate things. You may be able to insert it with an icon in the editor. But if not, just stick in <hr> to get a line.

<img> - Images

HTML identifies images by placing a link to the file of the image inside the <img> tag. This tells the browser to download the image and render it. In most cases your blogging platform editor handles images for you. If you are looking at the HTML, you should know what <img> is and change some basic settings if needed.

<iframe> - Embedded Content

If you want to stick a video, file, or something like an audio player into your blog post, you use the <iframe> tag. It tells the browser to go to another location and render whatever you find inside a box defined by the <iframe> tag. In most cases, you will just copy and paste <iframe>'s into your blog post. The site that generates the content will have an "embed" button that generates the <iframe> code. YouTube is a great example of this.

6. Dealing with Images - Tools and Techniques

As mentioned throughout this book, images are a great tool for conveying information and getting attention. The old adage that a picture is worth a thousand words still holds true in the age of the Internet. In most cases you can simply drag and drop an image file from your computer into your blog post and never touch it. The blogging editor will size it to the maximum size for the post and you are done. Most of the time this is actually the best way to go, especially in short posts.

The problem is that most of the time the images you have to work with are not "just right." They need to be cropped, maybe annotated to point something out, and in some cases run through a few filters to fix color or contrast. And that is where the trouble starts, you can spend more time editing one picture than it took to write the whole post. So use common sense and do just enough.

The most common mistake people make with images is to resize them and not keep the original aspect ratio. An image on a computer is made up of very small colored squares called pixels. By default, there are 72 pixels per inch. When you click on an image and drag the corner with your mouse to change its size you can change those squares into a rectangle, distorting your image. Even if that distortion is small, your readers will subconsciously notice it, and the strange aspect will throw them off. These days most software locks the aspect ratio, but be careful when you resize, you may need to hold down the shift key to lock the aspect ratio.

The tool you use for editing your blog posts most likely comes with a simple image editing capability, and for most cases it is all you need to rotate, crop, and resize your image. Get to know it so that you can quickly make changes when a picture just does not look right, and you need to chop something off or change it.

If an image is too dark, too light, or maybe you took it under fluorescent lights and the color is off, you can run some basic filters on it to clean it up. If you took the picture on your phone, just use the software on the phone to fix it. Your camera app should have basic filters and probably a super-duper default fixer-upper that you should just apply to every picture you take.

If you have gotten your images over to your computer then you have a couple of options. If you have Adobe Photoshop and you know how to use it, then you are more than good and you can do what is needed to prep images, annotate, and filter.

If you do not have Photoshop talk with IT to see what you do have. Both Microsoft and Mac operating systems come with simple editors that are probably good enough. Adobe also offers a free tool for computers and mobile devices called PhotoShop Express. It is a weak shadow of the full package but has all the tools you need to prepare images for a blog post.

If you need more, invest in Photoshop or search for "free image editing software" and see what the top recommendations are from a blog post or two. Right now, GIMP is a great free tool that has a lot of capability, far more than you need to prepare images for a blog.

One thing you may be tempted to do is play with some of the filters on social media that change your images to make them look old or more "artistic." Since you are doing a business blog and not sharing pictures of your bacon-infused bloody mary, it is probably not a good idea to use these tools. If you are an artistic person that knows how to actually make things look artistic, then go to it. Otherwise just put your images up with a little cleaning and cropping and go to town.

7. Tables

One of the most common items in a business blog, especially if it is for a technical industry, is a table. The problem is that none of the common blogging software tools come with a good table tool built in. Users of Microsoft Word know how easy it is in that tool to create a table and format it with colors and various line style. This can be done in HTML, but it is not simple and requires a lot of style coding. Not something you want to do regularly in your blog.

One simple solution is to do your table in Microsoft Word or Microsoft Excel and simply do an image capture of the table and save it, then include the image in your blog post. The downside of this approach is that the text in the table is not searchable. So if you think your readers will be searching for the content of the table, do not use this method or make sure you capture the same words in your text.

If you need your table as text in your post and you are not an expert at HTML, then your best choice is to use a plugin for your blogging system. WordPress has several, and as of this writing. TablePress is the most capable. Easy to use and feature-rich, it makes very professional looking tables without a lot of effort. There are also some online websites where you can build a table and generate the HTML that can be pasted into the HTML editor in your blogging tool.

As with everything we have talked about, the key here is to not get bogged down in making the perfect table. A good enough table can be built in a few minutes and conveys the information you want to share.

8. Style Attribute and Tag

You just cannot get your post to look right with the formatting tools built into your editor. You need more. Ask yourself if you really do. Are you sure? Still want to format more? OK, let's talk about the style attribute in HTML.

Early on in the days of HTML, it became clear that advanced formatting just was not possible with the basic controls that come with tags. Something better was needed. The clever solution was to stay within the existing HTML standard and add an attribute called style. The style attribute could then have a huge set of its own arguments that could be used to specify formatting. It works well and if you look at your HTML code you will see lots of inline style properties, or your objects will have a name or class associated with them that also refers to styles that are shared across the page and defined within a <style> </style>tag.

This topic should be, and is, its own book. If you want to add your own style arguments to your HTML to get better formatting you need to get a book or start learning from the Internet. Just remember to keep things simple and do not spend too much time on it. This book will cover the basics that you need to control critical things.

> Note: The reason why the formatting that these properties control are not found in the editor of most blogging tools is because you should not be mucking about with formatting too much. One thing that makes a blog look clean and professional is a consistent look and feel. If you are changing fonts, color, and size all the time, it just does not look as good.

Use style to highlight things that need highlighting or to clean up content that looks messy or is hard to follow. Nothing more.

Here are some basics that might come in handy. Look each of them up before you use them to understand how they work and what arguments they take.

Specifying Styles

There are two ways to attach a style to an HTML element: inline with the style attribute or across a page through a <style> tag. Inline is the simplest and easiest to implement on a blog and more importantly, it overrides any style specification that are applied to the site or the page. To use it you place:

```
style="name: value; name: value;"
```

Where "name: value;" pairs are called property declarations. As many of these arguments can be added as needed. The key thing to remember is that the name describes what you want to control, size, padding, color, etc... and it is followed by a colon. The value is the value you want to set what you want the thing you are controlling to be. It is a size, color, thickness, or some other descriptor. It is always followed by a semicolon.

As an example, if all of your <h1> headers are set to be black by the template you use for your blog, and you need one to be orange for some reason, you can override the black color definition with <h1 style="color: orange;">

The problem with inline style modifications is that you have to put them in for each and every element you want to control. If you need are of your <h1> elements to be green, then you would have to find each one and put <h1 style="color: green"> on each one. That is why the <style></style> tag exists.

Instead of putting property declarations on every element you specify what objects you want to control then specify name: value; for every instance of that object. The object can be all instances of a given tag, say all <h1>'s or you can define an id or class to apply it to. The <style> tag should go at the top of the HTML code for a blog.

The format is:

```
<style>
    tag
    {
        name: value;
        name: value;
    }
    .classname
    {
        name: value;
        name: value;
    }
    #idname{
        name: value;
        name: value;
    }
</style>
```

Where tag is HTML tag you want to effect, classname is the value of class="classname" you have applied to elements, and id is the value of id="idname"

If you are shaking your head and not following an of this, well you were warned. It is complicated. Stick with inline styles.

Here are the most important arguments to know.

```
Background: #color;
```

This defines the background color for the tag. Use it with <div> to make colored rectangles.

```
Color: #color;
```

The other thing you want to control the color on is your text. The color property does that and in most cases can be set in your editor. But if not, this is the property you use to do it in HTML.

```
Font-style: font-family;
```

When you need a different font you can sometimes set it in the editor. But in most cases the template for your blog sets the fonts. Use this to make a sentence or paragraph stand out by overriding the value set in the template.

```
Font-size: nnpx;
```

Along with the font and its color, you may want to change size. Again, this is not in most editors because you usually do not want to change font size. But if you need to, use this property with the desired size in pixels as the argument. 12px would be twelve pixels.

```
Margin: nnpx;
```

If things just look too cluttered on your post, a very easy and quick fix is to add a margin property to the style of whatever is getting too crowded. It takes the number of pixels as an argument. It is especially handing for images and <div>'s that just need some space around them. There is also margin-top, margin-bottom, margin-left, and margin-right if you just need space on one side of an object.

```
Padding: nnpx;
```

Padding is the opposite of margins. Margin is the space around the outside of an object. Padding defines the space that is to be left blank on the inside. Think of a box (a <div>) and you want space around the text inside that box. You can put a margin on the text or use padding on the <div>. It takes size in pixels as an argument.

```
Border: width style color;
```

The largest group of properties in style have to do with borders around an object. You can do a lot with borders. They are a great way to highlight or separate different pieces of content in a post.

Fortunately, the border property covers most needs. The first argument it takes is the width of the border in pixels. You can use words like thin or thick here as well. The next is style, which can be solid, dashed, double, etc... And finally, you give a color. Color can be a #rrryygg hex color or common names like black, red, yellow, etc...

```
Vertical-align: location;
```

How text is aligned horizontally can be controlled by the editor in your blogging tool. But if you have text inside something, it can also be aligned to the top, center, or bottom with this property. This property gets used a lot if you put text inside rectangles or tables.

More Options

There are hundreds of options for style. The best way to find one you want is to get very familiar with :

www.w3schools.com/css

Everything you need is listed there, and it includes a tool to try things out live. You can get what you want then copy and paste it into your HTML for your blog post.

9. The Sidebar

Most blogs use a standard layout that includes some sort of sidebar; an area on either side of the web page that stays the same from post to post. By default, it usually contains a list of most recent articles and a small "about" section. For a personal blog its purpose is to provide navigation and background. But for a business blog it is very important.

The whole reason why you are blogging is to get more revenue for our business. The content of the posts you put out there will attract people, and your skillful writing will hopefully spur them to some sort of action that will result in more sales. You also need to provide a place to give readers a chance to learn more and to take action – and that is how you should use the sidebar.

You may be tempted to stick advertising in the text of your posts. Do not. It is annoying and makes your posts look too much like you are selling. Place more subtle advertising and calls to action on the side.

The format should be simple. You can have a few advertisements, but not too many and not too bold. The bulk of the side content should be images and links to more information, to interacting with your team, or even to making a purchase.

Most blogging sites have some sort of a widget capability. Widgets are small formatting objects that you can arrange on your page, usually in the sidebar. You can use them to include search, a list of recent articles, and small HTML snippets for advertising and such. Take a look and play with them. Do not get too fancy and they will work well.

Make sure you explore and leverage what your sidebar can do, it really is the final step in interacting with your customers and if you do not use it, all of your great content may go to waste.

10. Getting Statistics

Statistics have become one of the fantastic fringe benefits of publishing content on the Internet. Tracking tools can tell you who clicked where, from where, and when. This type of information is interesting and either good or bad for the ego, depending on how well your content is getting noticed.

More importantly, it can be used to help you decide what is and what is not working on your blog. Historical data can simply identify which posts are viewed the most, search data can tell you what keywords are bringing readers to the site, and data on links that are clicked will show when people want more information. By looking at this fairly regularly, you can make informed changes to your topics and how you interact with readers within your posts.

Most blogging sites offer statistics, it's a standard feature in WordPress. Talk to your IT department and see if they have a preferred tool that they use for your whole website that you should use. You want to make sure you are tracking the number of visits to each post, what search keywords brought them to your site, and what links within your posts people are clicking on.

Either way, do not overdo it. But at the same time do not ignore statistics. If you are making an investment in a business blog, you should track how things are going and find out what works and what does not. It may also help you justify additional resources with management.

11. Plugins

Plugins are your best friends. They allow you to add little software tools to your blog without the need to program. They expand the basic capabilities of a blogging tool far beyond just a blogging platform. One of the reasons why WordPress is so popular is because of the huge library of free and paid plugins that are available on the platform, numbering in the tens-of-thousands. And better yet, they are all rated and have download statistics. This allows you to easily tell which work and are popular.

It is probably not a good idea to start right off with a bunch of plugins, but once your site is stable and you have a few posts under your belt, look at adding a few to improve things. Take a look at the most popular plugins and consider using them. Contact forms, anti-spam tools, and SEO tools. You can even add a simple e-commerce site or host a bulletin board.

Some of the most useful types of plugins are those that publish announcements about your posts to social media or let readers share your posts easily on social media. One of the higher rated versions of these two tools should be added early on.

Another great plugin for a business site is something that will display PDF files in a viewer on your blog. If you install one of these plugins you can display your converted documents, from brochures to PowerPoint presentations, right in the middle of your blog post. That way visitors do not have to download a file to see the content.

Another important family of plugins are for search. The built-in search tool may be pretty good, but the plugin search tools are much faster and more capable. Plus they present results in a format people are used to seeing.

Some sort of slideshow or animated viewing tool for images is another great way to spice up your posts with very little effort.

Take a look at what is available and play a little. Plugins are easy and add a lot of value. And they can be turned off in a click if you do not like them. If you ever feel like you need a capability that is missing, or that you need to hire a consultant to add something, look for a plugin first. What you need probably already exists.

12. Embedding Video and Document Content

Much of this book talks about the traditional blog content: text and images. However, a blog can support a large variety of content types including video and documents. Sharing this type of information is fairly easy and the only thing be careful of is to make sure it fits in nicely and does not look forced.

For video, your best bet is to publish your video content on YouTube. Once you have a link for the video you want on your site, simply paste the link to the video into your editor, and it will be recognized and displayed as an embedded video. If your editor does not recognize the link automatically, you will need to insert an embedded video as HTML. Fortunately, YouTube and most video services crate the HTML for you.

In YouTube simply click on the "Share" button then click "Embed." This shows an <iframe> tag with everything you need to embed. If you click "show more" you can even change the size. Stick the HTML <iframe> element into your HTML editor and it should show up in your post with no problem. If you do have a problem, search for information on the <iframe> tag and look for solutions.

A small trick if you are not familiar with HTML and have trouble figuring out where to put your video in that pile of code. In the standard editor, type "... video ..." where you want the video. Then go into the HTML editor and search for "... video ..." Select that text and paste the <iframe> element in its place.

There are plugins for video display, and you can host videos on your web server. If you wish to use either of these, it is recommended that you work with your IT provider or web services provider to set that up and make sure it is reliable.

For other types of documents, like PDF or Microsoft Office documents, you will need to use plugins. Try a couple to see which one works best. It is a really good idea to convert as much content to PDF as possible since this usually does not require anything special for people to view it. Remember, you want to make it simple for your readers to get to your content. PDF is the best way to do that.

It is often tempting to simply post a video or a document and call a post done. That is OK, but you need some text. Make sure you include descriptive words for the search engine and readers. Not a lot, but enough to tell either what the video or document is about.

PART 5: TIPS BECOMING A BETTER BLOGGER

Once you have started blogging you have done the most difficult part. Keeping that content coming over time is most of the battle and if you can do that, you have achieved more than most.

Once you get things going and you have a rhythm, do not stop working on getting good. You can be a better blogger if you make a little more effort and focus on improvement. This section goes over a few key suggestions to improve your blogging and your blog.

1. Look for Examples

Imitation is the sincerest form of flattery, so get out there flatter some people. Find some blogs in your industry, or on topics that interest you, and start to read them regularly. Learn from what they do right, and what they do wrong.

When you visit another blog ask yourself some questions:

- Does it have a good look and feel?
- What feels good and what feels bad?
- Is it easy to navigate and why?
- What made the post you are reading interesting or boring?
- Did you find a call to action or feel a desire to do business with the company? Why?
- What could you copy on your blog?
- What could you avoid doing on your blog?

You may want to take notes when you visit another blog. Another good tactic is to ask other employees who are not so buried in the mechanics of blogging to visit the same blog and give you their impressions.

It is fairly common to do this type of research when you start a blog. It is more important to keep doing it as your blog matures. The technology behind blogging improves, and the ways people use it evolve all the time. Stay on top of things and improve your blog.

2. Form a Support Group

Writing is a lonely business, and blogging is no different. Having others to talk things over with, bounce ideas off of, or just getting reassurance is very helpful. See if you have friends or business acquaintances that blog. Or reach out to bloggers that you read and like, they are struggling with the same things you are.

Take the initiative to form an informal support group. Maybe you just agree to communicate over email. Maybe you have regular online meetings. Whatever works for your group, leverage it. Do not underestimate the value of having people to talk to.

3. Reread Older Content

Just as you should be looking at the content of others to gain insight, you should critically review your own content. Every time you publish something you not only learn a bit more about publishing, but you put it out there in the world to get feedback. Taking a look in hindsight is powerful.

If you have statistics use them to find out what articles did well, and what did not. Then read them from the point of view of your prospective customer as well as from a business perspective. You are trying to find areas to improve future content.

As you look at each of the following aspects, take notes and use those notes when you create new content:

Look and feel

Review the formatting, where images are, how the content flows on the page. Does it look professional and will it appeal to customers? Go back and read the content in this book about look and feel and apply it to what you see. Then write down where you can make good changes.

Usefulness

Remember that the number one rule is to publish useful content often. In hindsight, is the content you are reviewing useful? Even if it was useful when you put it out there, is it useful now?

It is important to answer this question from the perspective of your audience. Did they have the information necessary to find value or should you have included more? Did you get to the point quickly enough or did you wander around a bit? Is it something that people can skim and get what they want?

Statistics could be helpful in understanding if the content was useful by simply checking to see if people are still reading it. Readership of a post should go down over time simply because there is newer information on the web. But if it dropped off a lot, odds are there was not a lot of value in the post. If it stays steady or goes up, you have provided something useful.

Effectiveness

After looking to see if you delivered value to your readers, it is time to see if there was any value to your company. Statistics will tell you if you had readers, but it will be a bit more difficult to assess if that interest turned into business.

Look at the content with hindsight. Did it reinforce your brand, did it promote your product, and did it include some sort of call to action. Go back and look at the goals you have for publishing and see if the article meets those goals.

Try and put yourself in the "typical customer" mindset and read the post. Does it make you want to do more business with your company? Does it pull you towards interacting or making a purchase? Does it give you ideas on how to use the products or services your company offers?

Execution

The last thing to check is your execution, or more specifically, how well the posts you are reviewing were written. If you did the writing, maybe you should have someone else take a look at this aspect.

Go back to the sections in this book about writing content. Were you following those guidelines? Do paragraphs contain complete ideas and do they flow one to another? Is your grammar good enough? Do the number of typos, yes you will find typos that have been there for a while, detract from the content?

The key thing to think about when it comes to execution is how you can do better. You have experience now. Spend some time thinking about how can you be more professional and more engaging in your writing.

Do a rewrite

A very useful exercise after rereading content is to pick a post and do it again. Use what you know now to see what you can do better. Then compare the two and see how you have done. There is no better way to gauge improvements and identify where you still need work than repackaging the same content. Find some piece of new information to add and publish it as new.

4. Raise the Bar

A common theme behind effective business blogging is that good enough is good enough and that you will waste time and money trying to get everything perfect. That does not mean that you should not have a high standard.

High standards are not just about formatting or impeccable sentence structure. For a business blog, it is about how often you publish, how useful your content is, and most importantly, how much business it drives.

Many business blogs fail because they are not given enough priority and they are treated as side projects. "Work on the blog when you have some downtime." However, your company's blog is a business publication, an informal publication, but still a business publication.

Raise the bar by taking the time to set goals, to review content before publishing, and to go out and find examples of how people are doing things better. It is more about being committed to publishing useful content often.

A commitment from senior management is critical as well to get serious attention from the rest of your company. One great way to achieve this is to have senior management blog, or at least be interviewed as part of the blog. Ghostwriting for the CEO and other senior people is very common. As long as they review and approve what is written, it is a fantastic a great way to get their involvement and leverage their position from a marketing perspective.

5. Other Random Ideas to Make Your Blog Better

There are dozens of ways to get better at blogging, and the previous sections covered the most important. Beyond that, here are some simple ideas that should help, presented in no particular order:

Titles of authors are important

Remember that in a business blog there is a very good chance that readers have absolutely no idea who your content authors are. This is a problem because you are trying to establish yourself as a credible resource, a trusted advisor. If they do not know that Bob Johnson has been studying watermelon breading for thirty-five years, then they may not be as trusting of his content.

You can include profiles or mini-biographies, but they only have an impact if a reader clicks on the link and reads it. A very quick and easy way to get that credibility is to include a title for your authors. The title should be their real title only if it conveys key information. If their title is Engineer II, then do not bother using their title. If it is Senior Customer Support Engineer, use that. For cases where the title is not impressive, you may want "special" titles for bylines. These can be titles that you come up with that describe the author or a simple sentence that conveys what you want.

Bob Johnson, Supply Chain Analyst 3 does not inspire loyalty. Bob Johnson, Senior Watermelon Procurement Expert, works much better.

You can include it in the byline, or have a brief blurb at the end of the post that has the name, title, and location of the author.

Do not forget the rules

The core of this book are the ten rules for successful business blogging. Review them regularly and use them.

1) Publish Useful Content Often
2) Minimize the Cost of Production
3) Readability, Not Perfection
4) Be Concise
5) Stick to One Topic or Message
6) Write for your Target Reader
7) Link to Details and Background Information
8) Keep it Informal and Conversational
9) Use a Hierarchy Structure
10) Use Examples and Images

Remember why you are doing a business blog

When you start blogging, especially if you are attempting to be informal and playful, it is easy to forget you are writing a business blog. The point of the whole effort is to sell more stuff. Do not alienate potential customers, do not have a negative impact on your brand. Work to get loyalty and encourage action from your readers.

Have fun

This is so important. If you are having fun on your blog, the audience will sense it and enjoy your content more. Even if you have decided to be serious and not use humor, enjoy the experience of learning and sharing information. Enthusiasm shines through and is a powerful way to improve your brand.

Do not buy or republish outside content

Once you start blogging you will get contacted by people who want to sell you content or want you to republish their content. This seems tempting but is a bad idea because you will not get what you want, which is content useful to your readers that improves your business. You will just be another website with manufactured content trolling for clicks.

Do not confuse republishing with publishing content from partners, customers, or vendors. That is fantastic and should not be considered "outside content."

Do consider hiring a professional

You can also pay someone to write, an actual professional. But they should be part of your organization or a close contractor that knows your company and your industry, not a service that churns out content. They should be good at not just writing, but at taking existing content or interviews with employees or customers and turning that into interesting posts.

The best way to make sure you have the right outside resource is to first review what they have already written. Is it at the standard you want, is it easy to read, and does it convey useful information? Writing fan fiction or even hard news stories is not the same thing as blogging for a business.

Then test them. Have the prospective writer take some existing content and turn it into a post or have them write up an event. Then ask them to interview someone and turn that into an article. Pay attention to the process as much as the final product. Were they on schedule? Did they work fairly independently? Was it more work to get them the information needed than if you had done it yourself?

Do not be shy about telling someone they are not a good fit if they are not a good fit. Move on to someone else. It may not happen on the first try, but the right writer for your blog is out there.

Training and Tutorials

A fantastic type of content to have on your blog is free training and tutorials. This is hard for some businesses, but if your customer base needs to know how to do something related to your product, you can do very well with this type of content because it is very popular.

How can you help your customers get more value out of the products you sell or learn how to do things related to your product or industry? It does not have to be specific to what you sell, it just has to be related and establish you as that domain expert.

Use Gated Content Wisely

One of the problems with sharing content on the Internet with customers is that if you just put it out there they access valuable information and you build loyalty, but you have no way of contacting them to follow up. To fix this you can set things up to give access to a download or to view some sort of content after your reader gives some basic contact information. This is called gated content. A form that they fill out before they can download what they want.

Sounds great on paper and it was very popular in the 2015-2016 time period, then it faded. For the simple reason that some people do not like to fill out forms. They do not want to give away information.

So use gated content wisely. It may work great, or it may stop people from seeing your content. You need to know your market and if people will give up contact information, which implies a sales call or emails, to get at the content. In some cases they will. But it is not that common. The key is to use this approach wisely and only with very valuable content.

Grammar Sites

One issue many people face when blogging is that they are not professional or trained writers, and they often get grammar wrong. As stated earlier, that is OK as long as it is not too much and it does not distract from the content.

But if you need to double-check and learn more, use the Internet. There are some very good grammar sites out there that can be found with a quick search.

betterbloggingforyourbusiness.wordpress.com

The companion blog to this book is also a resource you should regularly check. It will contain additional information that didn't make the book, links, and other useful content that will be published often.

6. Write

The best way to get better at writing is to write more. Few things improve your blogging faster than more blogging. As with any skill, practice makes what you are doing better, and this is especially true for writing. If you are doing the writing this applies to you. If you are the person coordinating things make sure the people who give you content just write a lot.

One way to make sure you write more is to make it easy to write. Back in the day, would-be authors could carry a notebook everywhere and jot in it when their muse spoke. These days we use computers so making sure you have a tablet or laptop so you can write at any time, goes a long way. Use a simple text editor and save the content in the cloud so you can get to it anywhere at any time. A pad with a Bluetooth keyboard is a nice portable solution and you may allready carry a pad with you everywhere already.

The next thing to do is to try and not put too much pressure on creating content. Simple little three-paragraph pieces are just as important as a one thousand word post with video and images. The important thing is to keep it coming. Every time you finish, you get better and more confident in your writing.

It is also not a bad idea to use writing prompts for yourself or those who write for you. "Four paragraphs on why seedless watermelons are sweater this year versus those from last year."

Writing just for your blog is not the only way to write more. If you have time, you can do practice pieces. Many websites have free writing prompts where you can create something and upload it for others to see. It is kind of fun and writing about things outside of your company's area of interest can be educational and a bit of a relief.

When you are done with something, it may not be publishable. Even if what you write is not usable, you can save it and edit it or rewrite it later. It is the process of putting words down that improves your skill. What counts is you are training your brain to convert thoughts and ideas into something of value.

7. Do it!

So what are you waiting for? Write something about what you learned at work today. Think about what got last got you excited about your job, or what trends in your industry keep you up at night, and start letting those words flow.

Go write something.

Publish useful content often!

ABOUT THE AUTHOR

Eric Miller is an engineer and small business owner based in Phoenix, Arizona. Most of his career has been spent using, selling, and supporting the advanced computer-based software and hardware that mechanical engineers use to design and manufacture products.

As co-owner of a small business, PADT, Inc, he oversaw the publishing of their newsletter for users of ANSYS Simulation software tools called "The Focus." When blogging came along the newsletter transformed into a blog, www.paditnc.com/blog, which sees an average of 50,000 visits a month. He has contributed over 500 posts to "The Focus" since its launch in 2010.

He is also a weekly guest blogger for The Phoenix Business Journal with over 100 posts on topics related to technology, startups, and running a small business. Regular contributions to other industry magazines and local business publications make up the remainder of his work related writing. Eric is often asked to speak on the same topics.

Most of his work day is spent running, with two partners, an 80 person engineering firm focused on providing products and services for simulation, product development, and 3D Printing.

Eric is honored to serve on the Board of Directors of the Arizona Technology Council and on the Board of Advisors of BioAccel. He enjoys travel, cooking, running (slowly), and taking part as a mentor and investor in the growing Arizona startup community.

www.ingramcontent.com/pod-product-compliance
Lightning Source LLC
Chambersburg PA
CBHW070250230526
45470CB00002B/556